A Breath of Fresh Air

A Breath of Fresh Air

Biblical Storytelling with Prisoners

AMELIA C. BOOMERSHINE

CASCADE *Books* · Eugene, Oregon

A BREATH OF FRESH AIR
Biblical Storytelling with Prisoners

Cascade Books
An Imprint of Wipf and Stock Publishers
199 W. 8th Ave., Suite 3
Eugene, OR 97401

www.wipfandstock.com

PAPERBACK ISBN: 978-1-61097-703-6
HARDCOVER ISBN: 978-1-61097-705-0
EBOOK ISBN: 978-1-61097-704-3

Cataloging-in-Publication data:

Names: Boomershine, Amelia C., author.

Title: A breath of fresh air : biblical storytelling with prisoners / Amelia C. Boomershine.

Description: Eugene, OR: Cascade Books, 2017 | Includes bibliographical references.

Identifiers: ISBN: 978-1-61097-703-6 (paperback) | ISBN: 978-1-61097-705-0 (hardcover) | ISBN: 978-1-61097-704-3 (ebook).

Subjects: LCSH: Bible—Study and teaching | Storytelling—Religious aspects—Christianity | Church work with prisoners | Prisoners—Religious life.

Classification: BV4340 B66 2017 (paperback) | BV4340 (ebook)

Manufactured in the U.S.A.   03/10/17

To Tom
With love and deep gratitude

There are vast numbers of valleys filled with dry bones in the world today, but for now let us turn our attention to the prisons, where a whole multitude of brothers needs that breath of life blown into them.
—GEORGE (LEO) DIAZ,
SING SING CORRECTIONAL FACILITY, 1998

Contents

Acknowledgments

Listen to the Word that God has spoken
Listen even if you don't understand
Listen to the One who began Creation
Listen to the One who is close at hand[1]

I ACKNOWLEDGE AND GIVE thanks to God for this book. It is an offering for the community in hopeful trust that it can be used by the Spirit for good.

I was standing in my study with Tom four years ago conversing about the Doctor of Ministry focus group he would soon be mentoring. A prospective student had just dropped out and there was some question about whether the group was viable. Suddenly, with more than a little exasperation, these words came out of my mouth: "Maybe I should do a project on biblical storytelling with people who are incarcerated and write a book about it!" Where those words came from, God only knows. But there was no taking them back. The inspiration may have been divine, but from start to finish, Tom, this book "is all your fault." Thank you.

Tom Boomershine is not only a pioneer in the field of biblical storytelling and performance criticism, but also my husband. We have been vocational as well as life partners for two decades. This book is a fruit of our work together. It was his conviction about the positive potential of biblical

---

1. Adaptation of "Listen to the Word that God Has Spoken," #455 in Eicher, *Glory to God*, music and words anonymous.

storytelling for people in prison that planted the seed for the "Breath of Fresh Air" project. In a myriad of ways, he is responsible for the existence of this book.

As faculty mentor, Lisa Hess provided general oversight of my doctoral process and specific evaluation of my written work. I am grateful for her careful reading of my documents, detailed feedback, and support in pursuit of publication. Our "Biblical Storytelling in Digital Culture" focus group was diverse, lively, positive, honest, and supportive. The group's encouragement for my work was invaluable. Many thanks to Kathy Culmer, Elizabeth Green, Meghan Howard, Joyce Johnson, Ron Poisel, and Brice Thomas.

Richard Boone shepherded my work at Chillicothe Correctional Institution from a variety of critical perspectives. His experience as a New Testament scholar, an elder in the United Methodist Church, and Program Coordinator for the Horizon Prison Initiative was a multi-faceted gift. Phil Ruge-Jones supported my learning from his base of expertise in theology, performance criticism, biblical storytelling, and pedagogy, with the added advantage of experience working with marginalized and incarcerated persons. Chaplain Willie Templeton was my mentor at the Montgomery County Jail. He shared generously of the wisdom he gained through seventeen years as a corrections officer and a lifetime of Christian ministry. Mary Hallinan drew on her experience and expertise regarding the criminal law system and spiritual direction to introduce me to the restorative justice movement, train me in peacemaking circle processes, and guide me in relating to incarcerated women.

Others who in various ways made significant contributions to the work that resulted in this book include: Tom Applegate, Susan Bennett, Barbara Blacklock, Jennifer Davis, Mel and Pat Enyart, Sherry Gale, Richard Green, Cortney Haley, Ellen Handlin, Beth Holten, Ezra Knox, Felicia LaBoy, Roberta Longfellow, Gye Miller, Myrna Miller, Sharlyn Radcliffe, Elizabeth Rand, Rhea Smith, Jim Vance, and Evette Watt. I appreciate each of you very much.

I give thanks for the men and women who participated in Circle of the Word at the Chillicothe Correctional Institution and the Montgomery County Jail over the past few years. I continue to be inspired by their thoughtful insights as together we engage the stories. I am impressed by their cooperation in trying new things, their willingness to share life experiences, and their heartfelt expressions of appreciation. I am deeply grateful for how fully they engage the Circle of the Word process, and how seriously they take the work I ask them to do in learning and telling biblical stories.

I am grateful to my stepmother, Shirley Cooper, who has believed in my ability to write since high school, and has encouraged me to write a book for almost that long. Her experience as a dissertation director at the University of Michigan came in handy as I struggled with the conundrum of research approaches. Her more recent experience as a volunteer working with community organizations enabled helpful conversation relevant to my project. Her conviction of the importance of the topic kept me writing when I was tempted to stop.

Finally, I would like to acknowledge and thank my three children: Genevieve, Dan, and Annabelle. Their enthusiasm for Mom pursuing an unexpected call and then writing a book about it has been a steady source of joy. I did not anticipate and could not have asked for three more lively advocates for my calling to do biblical storytelling with incarcerated men and women. Beloved children, you are the cheering squad for *A Breath of Fresh Air: Biblical Storytelling with Prisoners*.

Amelia C. Boomershine
Dayton, Ohio
July 2016

Introduction

THE GENESIS OF THE title for this book happened like this. I was sharing lunch with my son Dan at a sidewalk café on a beautiful fall day in Covington, Kentucky, just a few blocks from the Ohio River. He told me about the frustrating night he had at work in a local bar, then I told him about the work I just started in a prison and a jail. I mused aloud about whether or not a biblical storytelling approach to the scriptures would be a source of hope for the men and women incarcerated there. At a pause in our conversation he said something I only half heard: ". . . breath of fresh air." I looked around and breathed in the beauty of the fall day replying, "Yes, it's really great out today." "No," he corrected me, "YOU are a breath of fresh air." I looked at him in amazement. I felt that he had named a deep desire of mine and confirmed my new vocation.

Months later I sat in a locked, windowless classroom deep inside the county jail with two other church ladies and nine female inmates. We spent ninety minutes engaging the story of Jesus' death. It was early April, ten days before Good Friday. This was our sixth weekly session telling, learning, listening, and connecting with the passion narrative from the Gospel of Mark. Before we sang our closing song I asked what feedback they had about the class. One said, "Very helpful for my soul." Another said, "I learned things I didn't know, and it refreshed my memory of things I once knew." A woman, there for the first time that day, who was the mother of several children attending our church, said she got "detail about my higher power" and was grateful to meet "my kids' Bible study teachers." This was a surprising connection, but the most striking comment of all came from a young woman who simply said, "This time is like a breath of fresh air."

Introduction

The United States has the highest incarceration rate in the world with over two million of its citizens behind bars.[2] Many women and men are incarcerated as a direct or indirect result of the criminalization of select drugs such as heroin, cocaine, and marijuana through the so-called "War on Drugs." Injustices associated with this war are well documented. The historic oppression of African Americans has continued through this system of mass incarceration.[3] Prisons have been places more frequently geared for retribution, rather than rehabilitation or restoration. The current trend of prison privatization has exacerbated these problems.

The financial and human cost of mass incarceration is very high at both the individual and communal levels. Recidivism rates soar with nearly a third of those incarcerated returning to jail or prison within five years of release. In the words of a jail chaplain, "People are serving life sentences in installments."[4] Most people who are incarcerated are victims themselves, as well as victimizers, caught up in a cycle of poverty, abuse, and criminality that is as difficult to escape as any bricks and mortar prison.

How does the body of Christ respond to this complex web of human tragedy? Clearly there is a need for the church to engage in social action to address the systemic injustices that caused and maintain mass incarceration. The church needs to function in its prophetic role. At the same time, there is the need for grass roots ministry with specific individuals in specific institutions, fulfilling Jesus' mandate to visit those in prison (Matt 25:31–46). If the church's work is informed and empowered by the breath of God, those who follow one inmate's exhortation to "Do *something*"[5] can act with confidence that they are in concert with God's will whether their approach is systemic or grass roots.

This book presents a grass roots approach to a pervasive problem. The approach, called "Circle of the Word," grew out of an intuition that

2. The U.S. Department of Justice reports that at yearend 2013 the number of inmates in state and federal prisons and local jails was 2,220,300. Glaze and Kaeble, "Correctional Populations in the United States, 2013," 2.

3. Michelle Alexander makes the case for mass incarceration as a new form of systemic racism. Alexander, *The New Jim Crow*.

4. Willie Templeton, Jr. at a Volunteer Chaplain Meeting, June 2014.

5. During a three-day immersion experience at an Ohio state prison, a group of United Methodists from around the country invited the "men in blue" to give their recommendations for positive action. The men presented a thoughtful list of varied suggestions. Their spokesman concluded the presentation with the tag line, "Do *something*," which quickly became a catchphrase for the group.

xiv

the behemoth of mass incarceration could be challenged through the convergence of biblical storytelling pedagogy, restorative justice principles, and peacemaking circle structure. Circle of the Word was developed and tested with men in a state prison and women in a county jail. This research demonstrated that the Circle of the Word model nurtures hope for meaningful life among incarcerated men and women. Furthermore, it enables church members to be in incarnational relationship with people directly impacted by the criminal justice system. It can truly be a breath of fresh air blowing through the gates and bars of the oppressive American criminal justice system.

Millennia ago, Aristotle and Cicero identified the role of human breath in effective speech.[6] The prophets of Israel and the evangelists of the early church recognized the role of divine breath in salvation. Grounded in telling the stories of God, Circle of the Word could well be a means of breathing the Holy Spirit into prisoners so that they may live. It may be, in the words of Bryan Stevenson, "a very simple intervention"[7] to transform both lives and prisons. My hope in writing this book is to provide a compelling foundation in scripture, history, theology, and theory, so that others will establish Circle of the Word in their communities.

I begin this book by sharing enough of my own story for you to gain a sense of my personal perspective, and to know the sources of motivation for my work with people who are incarcerated. This social placement is intended to assist in making your own evaluation about the material I present and the claims I make. Perhaps you will find points of congruence with your own experience, as well as points of departure. Either should make your reading more meaningful.

Chapter 2 introduces a trio of practices: restorative justice, peacemaking circles, and biblical storytelling. Restorative justice is in contrast to retributive justice, which characterizes the American criminal justice system. The chapter will begin with a brief look at this system and its underlying philosophy. Peacemaking circles, inspired by Native American talking circles, are a core practice in restorative justice work. Circle of the Word is structured by the form and spirit of the peacemaking circle model. Its content is engagement with a biblical story; hence the name, Circle of the Word. I conclude chapter 2 with an overview of biblical storytelling as an

---

6. Lee and Scott, *Sound Mapping the New Testament*, 108–9.

7. Bryan Stevenson, *Just Mercy*, 17.

ancient-contemporary practice of spiritual formation, and of biblical sto-rytelling workshops which engage specific stories in a small group setting.

Circle of the Word is a spiritual empowerment experience centered on specific biblical stories. Those who undertake development of their own Circle of the Word will need the resource of a new paradigm of biblical study as they work with the stories from the biblical tradition. The first part of chapter 3 introduces a twenty-first-century hermeneutic called "perfor-mance criticism." I summarize what it is, how and why it developed, and why it is important.

In the second part of chapter 3, I describe specific processes of "ex-periential exegesis"—Bible study that seeks experience of the scripture as closely as possible to the way in which the original audiences experienced it. I detail these processes because many of them will be unfamiliar, since traditional theological education is wedded to the old paradigm of study-ing the Bible as text. Acquaintance with experiential exegesis clarifies how distinctive Circle of the Word is compared to the type of biblical study commonly offered in jails and prisons. It also helps facilitate the necessary interpretive skills for Circle of the Word preparation.

The following chapter applies these exegetical processes to two stories that are foundational for Circle of the Word ministry. Both of the passages tell about the Spirit of God breathing on God's despairing people to give them new life, to fill them with hope, and to empower them for mission. The first passage treated is the prophetic story of "Dry Bones" from Ezekiel 37:1–14. The second is the resurrection story "Behind Locked Doors" from John 20:19–23.

Historical foundations for Circle of the Word are presented in chapter 5. This chapter recounts the ways in which the Christian community in En-lightenment England tackled issues of imprisonment in the eighteenth and nineteenth centuries, including the issue of providing fresh air—literally—to prisoners suffering from its absence. The chapter begins by describing the work of Mr. Shute and the SPCK (Society for Promoting Christian Knowledge), the Wesleys and early Methodism, and John Howard, an Anglican layman. The chapter then focuses on the remarkable Quaker re-former, Elizabeth Fry. Her story serves as a model and inspiration to all those hearing Jesus' call to visit those in prison. The conviction, challenges, and achievements of the church through all these English Enlightenment Christians inform and inspire the church as it addresses comparable prob-lems in contemporary America.

An exploration of the doctrine of the Word of God in chapter 6 grounds Circle of the Word theologically through an effort to understand and describe relationships between the Word of God and biblical storytelling. The phrase "Word of God" means different things to different people. Examining its meaning through church history as well as its use by contemporary theologians illuminates the potential significance of biblical storytelling for people who are incarcerated and for those who minister with them.

In chapter 7 I turn to the social sciences for a theoretical foundation, drawing on theory and research in the new field of positive psychology. The goal of positive psychology is to answer an old question: "What makes a good life and a good person?"[8] Hope is part of the answer. Hope is an intangible yet essential aspect of human experience. Imprisonment severely strains the capacity for hope. Following an introduction to positive psychology and research on positive emotions, this chapter examines hope theory. What is gleaned through a study of hope from the perspective of positive psychology resonates with biblical narrative and shapes the design of Circle of the Word.

It is all very well to have a hunch that a particular approach to a given problem might be helpful, but before going very far in advocating that approach, it seems like a good idea to try it out in a systematic study. Chapter 8 documents research that tested Circle of the Word with incarcerated men and women in two detention venues. The testing project was named "Breath of Fresh Air." The project sought to discover what impact a Circle of the Word program would have on incarcerated men and women. Specifically, it explored the extent to which engaging the story of Jesus' passion, death and resurrection would be a source of hope. Chapter 8 describes the Breath of Fresh Air project and reports on its results.

If you are reading this book you may well be a student of the rabbi who put visiting prisoners high on his list of requirements for satisfactory completion of his discipleship course. I am guessing that you are either a layperson or a pastor with interest in detention ministry, or a chaplain. Perhaps you are an ecclesiastical leader or on the faculty of a seminary. You may be a former or current prisoner yourself, or a family member. Whatever your role, my goal in writing this book is to empower you to form a Circle of the Word in your local community and challenge mass incarceration at the grass roots.

8. Snyder and Lopez, *Oxford Handbook of Positive Psychology*, 8.

Toward that end, chapter 9 provides a blueprint for planning and implementation. It offers enough detail to get you started. Online resources are available as a supplement to this book to support the development of your Circle.[9] The book concludes by identifying the conclusions and possibilities of this research. It will take many Circles of the Word to significantly impact mass incarceration. On the other hand, it is amazing what God can accomplish with just a handful of courageous disciples filled with the fresh air of the Holy Spirit's breath and these sacred, empowering stories.

9. http://www.circleoftheword.gotell.org.

1

My Story

ROOTS

I WAS BORN AND raised in Big Ten college towns during the fifties and sixties. They provided a safe, yet stimulating climate in which to grow up. My father was a university professor of education administration, my mother a social worker. My father was a classic liberal. His concern for justice and poverty may have been fostered by experiences of the Great Depression as a young man attending college in Chicago. He told me about the lines of men out of work, waiting for soup and bread. In various ways during his career as an educational administrator he served those on the margins.

My mother was raised in Colorado and was deeply influenced by her grandfather, a United Brethren elder who evangelized settlers from high in the Rockies all the way to Denver. As a social worker my mother placed orphans in foster care in Chicago and then in Iowa City,s where I was born. In the early sixties she directed Planned Parenthood in Ann Arbor, Michigan. A cover article in a national magazine about "The Pill" quoted my mother. My mother thought effective, safe birth control was an important option for women, and far preferable to the dangers of illegal abortions.

I am proud of my parents for the work they did and grateful for the values they passed on to me. These values were grounded in Christian ethics. My family was mainline, liberal Protestant to the core. We were regular in church attendance and participation, as were many middle-class families in the American Midwest at that time. Religious practice in church was taken for granted. It was a different day.

SPIRITUAL FOUNDATIONS

When I was young our family attended First Methodist Church in West Lafayette, Indiana. My father was not much for ritual. He liked preaching, but not communion. I liked communion, but not preaching. To me the sermon was a painfully long time you had to sit still, be quiet, and listen to an incomprehensible monologue. In contrast, communion, though an infrequent practice in mid-century Methodism, was mysterious, participatory, and meaningful.

My parents' spirituality was actualized more in their concern for social justice than in liturgy or piety. I remember a time after church we drove down to see the shanty-town along the banks of the Wabash River. I was so uncomfortable I hid in the back seat of our big, white 1957 Lincoln. When I reflected on this experience years later, I wondered how it was for people living in those shanties to see our fancy car driving down their dirt road. But I also realized the concern and compassion that motivated my parents' Sunday drive through their neighborhood. My parents were not afraid of the poor. They planted the seeds of my own advocacy for people of limited means. They prepared me to embrace liberation theology and Jesus' "option for the poor" when I heard about them years later.

My father read the Bible at breakfast, at least for a while. That ended one Saturday morning, not too long after we got our first television. We were one of the last families in the neighborhood to own a TV because my father disapproved. Among other complaints he said it was too violent, especially the cartoons. Of course he was right about that, but I did not appreciate his view at the time. After making this critique one Saturday morning he insisted I turn off the television. We sat down to breakfast and my father read the Bible, as was his custom in those days. It happened that we had come to the story about Jael hammering a tent peg into the head of an enemy king. So ended our breakfast Bible readings, and also complaints about cartoon violence. I forgot about Jael—and also the breakfast Bible readings—until many years later when I once again encountered her story in the book of Judges. The sudden strength of connection with my past, my father, and the Bible surprised me. The Bible would prove to be an endless source of amazement.

Christmas was my introduction to Jesus. Every December we got out a set of ceramic crèche figures and a wooden stable. I arranged them under the tree. The figures had been hand painted by a relative of my father. They were fun to arrange and intriguing to contemplate. Another Christmas tradition was "Amahl and the Night Visitors." I loved both the story and the music. It helped form my early impressions of grace, faith, and Jesus.

That impression was reinforced by the movie "Ben Hur"—one of a handful of movies I saw during my childhood. There is an episode in which Judah ben Hur, unjustly condemned by his Roman friend to life as a galley slave, is denied the water he desperately needs to survive a forced march to the sea. A villager bends down to offer a full ladle of water and a soldier begins to rebuke him. We do not see the face of the villager, only his back, but we do see the face of the soldier. It is contorted with harshness as he barks his rebuke. The villager doesn't say a thing, but when he looks up, the soldier stops midsentence. The expression on his face changes from hostility to confusion, and culminates in a classic expression of being awe-struck with "fear of the Lord." The now speechless soldier backs off, allowing Judah to drink from the proffered ladle. The musical score leaves no doubt that the villager is Jesus.

The scene from "Ben Hur" formed my image of Jesus as one with the power to stop cruelty in its tracks and with the compassion to save those in need, whether they looked to him for help or not. I believed then that Jesus was for real and was in some way different from every other human who had ever lived. I understood him as different—not in a showy, loud way—but in a quiet, mysterious, and holy way. Along with shaping my view of Jesus, the fact that my spiritual life could be so influenced by a movie taught me the power of a story well told.

I took piano lessons as a child. I amused myself playing pieces from the music books we had lying around the house. One of my favorite books was a collection of folk music, and one of my favorite pieces in that collection was "Go Down, Moses." There were other spirituals in the book. I played them all. I think I learned more Bible from those spirituals than I did at church. I was impressed by the faith they expressed and was drawn by the history they reflected.

Our family valued and enjoyed the natural world. Gardening, camping, traveling, fishing, and animals were ways we interacted with the environment. With two of his colleagues in the Department of Education at Purdue, my dad purchased a twenty-eight acres peninsula on Lake

Superior, sixty miles north of Sault St. Marie. We would go up there every August to camp. August was about the only time of year we could enjoy it. Before August the black flies are vicious; after August it is cold. But during that one month, our Lake Superior land was magical, a little taste of heaven. Camping trips there provided some of the most wonderful times of my life, experiencing nature in all its glory. My earliest recalled experience of God was on that land, sitting on high rocks, looking down at the waves crashing below and out over the endless lake. I knew God was real, powerful, good, and wondrous.

While I was in high school my father took me to a large meeting of Arab students at the University of Michigan. We went with his doctoral student from Egypt. The keynote speaker was Stokely Carmichael and the topic was Black Power. It seemed that my father and I were the only white Americans in the audience. It was a consciousness-raising experience. Dad and I were in Chicago after Dr. King was assassinated and experienced the resulting turmoil there. In Ann Arbor we were close to the burning of Detroit. I read *The Invisible Man*, *Black Like Me*, and *The Autobiography of Malcolm X*. The year after I graduated, my high school went on "partial martial law" because of racial tension.

These events of my youth made a strong impression and developed my concern for racial justice. Dr. Martin Luther King, Jr. is the prophetic person of faith I came to admire above all others. His steadfast belief in the power of divine love and his courageous commitment to non-violent resistance to evil grew out of his deep knowledge of biblical stories. It was grounded in his experience and trust in the risen Christ. It reflected persevering hope that, despite all appearances to the contrary, justice would eventually triumph over fear.

I attended the University of Colorado during the Vietnam war. I participated in a candlelight march to protest the bombing of Cambodia. I became disillusioned with our president and government, and impatient with my father's acceptance of American policy. Dad had taken me to see Lyndon Johnson speak at the University of Michigan football stadium in May of 1964. In that speech, Johnson detailed his plans for the "Great Society." Comprehensive legislation followed such as the Civil Rights Act of 1964 that outlawed discrimination on the basis of race, color, religion, sex, or national origin, and the Social Security Amendments of 1965 that created Medicare and Medicaid. But by 1970, Johnson's vision was buried under the devastation of an unjust war. I joined the protests against military recruitment on campus and participated in a candlelight walk following the bombing of Cambodia.

It seemed to me that the Christians I knew in college had no problem with the war in Vietnam or campus ROTC. I was largely ignorant of the role that Christian faith played in the civil rights and anti-war movements, though significant branches of American Christianity did not support either.[1] I was interested in spiritual things—Buddhism, transcendental meditation, midnight Mass on Christmas Eve—but I remained by and large unimpressed with the church. This would change in the years to come when I re-entered the faith community as a young adult.

PREVENIENT GRACE

My parents separated when I was thirteen. One May night the next year I came home after a weekend up north with my father. The house looked strangely dark. As my father parked to drop me off I asked him to wait, sensing something was wrong. I went inside and found my mother upstairs in bed. I couldn't rouse her. We called our neighbor who was a doctor. An emergency crew came and pumped her stomach, but it was too late. She died from an overdose of barbiturates. There was a note my mother had written to us. The police took it away.

The most steady and reliable source of personal support during my youth and adult life was the woman my father married the summer before my senior year in high school. She had been the one on whom I projected all my angry pain about my mother's death. Yet she became not just a friend, not just family, but a trusted mentor. Throughout my life she has been there for me with advice and counsel, encouragement and comfort. Through my relationship with my stepmother I have experienced how God acts to bring goodness out of tragedy and transforms the spirit, sometimes even without invitation. I experienced the redemptive power of God and the prevenient grace manifested in our lives through people who care.

---

1. See Toulouse, "Christian Responses," for a detailed discussion of Christian responses to American involvement in Vietnam.

VOCATION

In the 1980s I married, moved to Cincinnati, and raised three children. During this time, I joined Hyde Park Community United Methodist Church. I became active in United Methodist Women and the committee on Church and Society. I taught Sunday school and chaired the Christian Education committee. I was mentored by the Director of Christian Education who encouraged me to seek ordination. She and two pillars of the church nurtured my passion for issues of peace and justice and shepherded my growing involvement with the institutional church.

A two-year Bethel Bible study introduced me to biblical study, which led to participation in Walk to Emmaus #9, Table of Deborah. This was a key turning point in my faith journey. At the Walk I came to understand God as love, not as judge or taskmaster. At the end of our Walk there was a "Dying Moments" communion service. "Pilgrims" were invited to come to the altar rail and leave something. I came to the rail and offered my doubts. It was not a decision to blindly believe everything about Christianity that was taught or to refrain from questioning. What I offered was resistance to belief that had been like a wall sealing me in. This wall of doubt prevented enjoyment of God, relationship with Jesus, and acceptance of the church as a viable institution worthy of commitment. I gave it up and left it at the altar. I made space for God to do a new thing in my life. That evening during a quiet time I went outside. It was cool, fall weather with a misty drizzle. I stood under a small tree in a courtyard. There I experienced Jesus' presence with me.

After my Walk I wondered where my new-found spiritual energy would lead. Direction came from a conversation with an elderly man whom I had gotten to know on my father's farm. My stepmother and I drove to visit him in Virginia. After dinner he took us aside and gave an impassioned plea that we address the issue of nuclear war. I took him very seriously, but had no idea what to do. That summer the School of Christian Missions happened to have a study on peace. I was off and running in a direction that eventually led to ordination.

In my thirst to know how and where the church was addressing such issues I attended more conferences and workshops. I went to General Conference in St. Louis and a conference on faith and justice in Chicago. I was present to hear Archbishop Desmond Tutu speak at a missions conference in Louisville. I went to a workshop at the Methodist Theological School in Ohio. It was sponsored by the West Ohio Annual Conference task force on

Peace and World Order, of which I was a member. That was my first biblical storytelling workshop. We learned the story of Jesus and the Syro-Phoenician woman as a way into the experience of reconciliation with enemies. Over the next few years biblical storytelling became my primary practice of spiritual formation. It has been the unifying theme in the various manifestations of my vocation for the past twenty-five years.

SHEOL

Two years attending Louisville Presbyterian Theological Seminary and another two at United Theological Seminary earned me a Master of Divinity degree. Upon graduation, I took off with my husband and three children for a sabbatical year in Cary, North Carolina. I was in the ordination process for the United Methodist Church, but decided after four years in seminary to postpone the last stages for a year, for the sake of re-grouping with my family. It was an ironic decision. We re-grouped, but not the way I expected. My marriage effectively ended that year.

Those nine months in Cary turned out to be what I came to call my time in Sheol. Without faith in God, the ministry of the church, and the discipline of biblical storytelling, I think my spirit might have died along with my marriage. One night I questioned my faith in God, a faith my spouse did not share. Was he right and I wrong? Then I literally cried out, "Don't let me lose my faith. I may lose all else, but I can't survive without my faith!"

I had a spiritual director, a nun in Durham. She helped me pray with Mary, the mother of Jesus. Mary, like myself, had to wait while facing an uncertain future. Sr. Chris also directed me to Psalm 139: "Where can I go from your spirit? Or where can I flee from your presence? If I ascend to heaven, you are there; if I make my bed in Sheol, you are there." Once while I was telling her what was going on in my personal life I suddenly lamented, "How can this be happening? I've done everything right all my life!" I stopped, having heard what I had just said. I knew, then, how pervasive in my spirit was self-righteousness. In this eye-opening moment, God answered my prayer not to lose faith. Moreover, God gave me hope to grow in faith.

Another time, as I walked through the woods in Cary, listening to a lecture I had on tape from a New Testament Introduction course, I saw a butterfly dancing in the sunlight. It was a sign of resurrection to me. It was

God's personal message that something good would come in my life, that I would be happy again one day.

God was present with me in many ways that year. The church and its people came to my assistance. Both the faith community at Duke Chapel and at First United Methodist Church in Cary welcomed and supported me. I experienced how the church can guide a person through hard times, bringing hope and encouragement.

GO AND TELL

I moved back to Cincinnati in June of 1992, in a state of marital separation that eventually resulted in divorce. I was unprepared for this change and full of anxiety, both for myself and for my children. The future looked bleak and I did not know what to do. I had a friend, Weldon Nisly, who was a Mennonite pastor for whom I had great respect as a man of deep integrity. Weldon and I were in a small guild of biblical storytellers. He was active in promoting peace and justice. Inspired by a call to boundary-crossing made in an address to the Network of Biblical Storytellers, he helped organize a biblical storytelling trip to the Soviet Union.

One day I went to Weldon and told him how afraid I was all the time. I asked him, "What should I do?" And he answered, "Stay close to Jesus." Coming from someone else I might have dismissed this answer as too simplistic, but coming from Weldon it meant everything. I clung to that thought and brought it to mind when fear overwhelmed me. Learning and telling myself biblical stories became the main way in which I stayed close to Jesus. Telling them to others gave me an experience of empowerment and awareness of the Spirit at work, right here and now, no matter what else was going on in my life or the world.

Thus began the last two decades of my life, in which the internalization and telling of biblical stories played the central role in my spiritual and vocational life. I began a series of jobs that brought together biblical storytelling and digital culture. I was a research assistant for the American Bible Society's Multimedia Translation Project, Coordinator for the Network of Biblical Storytellers, and Assistant Director of Christianity and Communications at United. I was Associate Pastor of Mason United Methodist Church for two years where I integrated biblical storytelling into local church ministry. During that time I married again and resolved to focus my ministry on biblical storytelling.

Together my husband Tom and I established a not-for-profit corporation called GoTell Communications whose mission is to equip people to discover and tell biblical stories as a spiritual discipline for embodying Jesus' way of peace in the world. Since its incorporation in 1998 I have served as Director. This work has involved production projects, presentations, and educational missions to cities in the United States and around the world. The position has embraced work for Coad Media in the United Kingdom, UMR Communications in Dallas, local churches, and the Network of Biblical Storytellers, International.

LIGHT IN DARKNESS

There are many ways in which my three children have shaped and strengthened my spirit and deepened my relationship with God. These include experiences of grateful joy at the gift of their lives, delight and wonder as I watch them grow, dependence on faith to endure the pain of their struggles, and humility caused by the challenges of parenting.

The hardest parental challenge I faced was the thirteen-month incarceration of my son. His stepfather and I were in Florida, having just completed a lecture tour, when the call came that my twenty-year-old had been arrested and was locked up in the Hamilton County Jail in Cincinnati. It was the darkest night of my life. Tom told me Psalm 23 and coached me to recite it for myself over and over again. That was how I survived the night and the days to come. Throughout the following months, the psalms informed the letters I wrote my son and gave him strength to endure his time in prison.

The arrest, trial, and visits in jail and prison were hard experiences of an alien world. They took me into unwelcome places of sorrow, shame, and remorse. But the Spirit of God was there, too. Whatever he had done, I still loved my son very much. And I knew he needed me. I found we could be in relationship through letters and visits. I came to understand more about how God loves us. Whatever we do, wherever we are, God adapts to meet us as we are. Like Paul, I came to be convinced, "neither death, nor life, nor angels, nor rulers, nor things present, nor things to come, nor powers, nor height, nor depth, nor anything else in all creation, will be able to separate us from the love of God in Christ Jesus our Lord" (Rom 8:38–39). There is always light in the darkness.

CHILDREN'S MINISTRIES

Throughout my thirty plus years of active church involvement, both as a layperson and as clergy I have been involved in Christian Education with children. I have been a Sunday school teacher, Chair of Christian Education, Children's Worship leader, and Vacation Bible School coordinator. I have taught biblical stories to children in Cambodia, Cameroon, and America. I have written several curricula to accompany *The Storykeepers* animated video series. I have led Children's Moments in worship, Musikgarten in a Y child care center, Backyard Bible club in the neighborhood park, and a biblical storytelling after-school program in a local elementary school.

In 2009 I became Director of Children's Ministries at Grace United Methodist Church in Dayton, Ohio. It was challenging, energizing, and in many ways the fulfillment of a lifelong call to work with children. But it was not the last stop on my vocational journey. Ministry with children at Grace led me to biblical storytelling with prisoners.

PRISON MINISTRY

One evening after a Wednesday night Kids' Club, I was walking down the hallway with a nine-year old who regularly attended Grace. She was an alert and thoughtful child, a good student, and a positive presence in our community of children. She lived with her grandmother whom I had come to know and respect. As we walked along, she mentioned her mother and I asked her whereabouts. She told me her mother was in the army.

Soon afterwards her grandmother told me that the mother was actually in prison. She said that her granddaughter was ashamed to tell me the truth. She said it had happened while I was overseas on a mission trip. Now the mother had been taken from prison to the county jail for a court appearance. Grandmother wished a pastor would visit.

I heard that wish as a call from God. I did not know where the jail was or how to go about a clergy visitation, but I found the jail downtown without much trouble and learned how to get authorized for pastoral calls. Thanks to fast action on the part of the Board of Ordained Ministry, that afternoon I went back for a visit. The "non-contact" visiting place was empty. It was a little room with two metal stools facing two thick windows, with cubicles on the other side of the windows and handsets to communicate. I was unsure what to do. Should I notify someone I was there? Should I go through the door next to the windows? I did not know whether the young woman I had come to visit would even want to see me. I sat down on a stool and waited.

She came before long and I introduced myself. She was distressed, afraid, and confused. She did not understand why she had been transported from the prison to the jail. She cried. I did not know what to say. I felt inadequately prepared for pastoral conversation, but I trusted that I was supposed to be there and stumbled along asking a question or two. I listened and tried to understand her words which was difficult because of her emotion and our different patterns of speech.

After the visit, a flood of memories came back from the time I visited my son in the Hamilton County Jail. I remembered the barren room with handsets and metal stools. I remember the pain of not being able to hold my son as he cried. I remembered having to leave him there, alone with his sorrow and remorse. They were painful memories, but I allowed them to inform my present rather than to rule it. I knew that the experience with my son would now prove useful. It was a sign of God's hand in things, for I believe God works like that—coaxing value out of the messes we make in life.

The following week at Kids' Club, the nine-year-old and I talked about my visit with her mother. It was a good talk. She wanted to know how her mother was. I told her she was sad and missed her. She wanted to know if I thought she looked like her mother. I said, "Yes, you are pretty like your mother." The next time I visited her mother was after she returned to the Dayton Correctional Institution. It had been converted just months before from a men's prison to a woman's prison in order to accommodate the growing population of female felons. We visited in the same room where I had visited my son a dozen years before. It was a strange feeling. I knew the place and more or less what to expect, so I was comfortable with the process of visitation there. But I was in for some surprises.

Initially the thing that surprised me was the way in which my ministry with children, which had been so joyful for me and so fruitful for the church, had brought me to this place that intersected in a powerful way with one of the hardest experiences of my life. I would never have guessed that such a difficult time could one day be empowering. I had learned during my son's year of incarceration that even in prison there can be laughter and joy in relationship—that love is not stopped by bars, guards, or razor wire.

I had learned that I could manage the intimidating atmosphere of jails and prisons. I knew that the Holy Spirit was just as active in the prison as anyplace else. If ever there was a place where the Word of God was needed, this was that place. In going to the prison, I had a strong sense of God's presence and guidance, of being led and not worrying about what happens next, or what I should say, or what I should do.

One day the church received a letter from the mother of two children who had come to Grace with their grandmother for breakfast on Sunday morning. I had helped them get involved in children's ministries by providing transportation. But suddenly they stopped attending. When I went to their house for a visit, neighbors said they had left, but had no idea where they had gone. The letter we received nearly a year later from their mother explained that she was in prison. She had gotten the address for Grace from the mother of the nine-year-old. In her letter to our church she wrote the name and phone number of the guardian who had custody of her children. She asked if we would bring them to church again.

We didn't have that many children attending Grace, about twenty at the time. How could it be that two mothers out of such a small group were incarcerated? When I thought about it, I realized more than two had parents behind bars. Others had fathers in prison. We were experiencing the impact of mass incarceration well before we heard it named. This harsh reality of the culture into which our children were born took on flesh and bones and reared its ugly head.

In September of 2011, Larry Lane, the chaplain of the Montgomery County Jail, gave a presentation at the Cincinnati-Dayton Guild of the Network of Biblical Storytellers. He explained why he chose to work with people in jail. One of his motives was pragmatic, the other spiritual. The pragmatic motive was that almost everyone in jail, sooner or later, will return to the community. It would be better for society if they returned more whole and healthy rather than less.

His spiritual motive was the parable of the sheep and the goats in Matthew 25: "for I was sick and you took care of me, I was in prison and you visited me." These words of Jesus conclude the recorded history of Grace Church.[2] They are also a reminder of John Wesley's mandate to his followers to visit in prisons, as he himself regularly did. A seed was planted for my vocation in prison ministry.

2. *Pilgrims of Grace, Volume II.*

September 2011 was also the occasion for my initial involvement with biblical storytelling in a state prison. Late in the month Grace celebrated its Bicentennial. The keynote speaker was a retired United Methodist bishop, the Rev. C. Joseph Sprague, who grew up in Dayton. In his talk, Bishop Sprague described the "pipeline to prison" for African American boys who cannot read at grade level by third grade. This caught my attention since I had initiated our church's involvement in a "Reading Buddies" program at the nearby neighborhood school. We worked with third grade boys who could hardly read at all. Were these young ones headed for prison?

The bishop also mentioned an interfaith residential program for incarcerated men called the Horizon Prison Initiative. The outcome of post-keynote conversation was an invitation to join a group exploring development of an academic program for Horizon graduates. My husband and I were interested in exploring the possibility of including a course on biblical storytelling. Subsequent sessions with the "men in blue" at an Ohio state prison were powerful experiences of the Spirit of God hard at work in the world, seeking to transform lives. The quiet faith of the planning team as well as the articulate faith of the men in blue was inspiring. I felt, as I did at the jail and the women's prison, that this was a place where I had something meaningful to offer and also where I would receive something meaningful.

The convergence of these varied circumstances relating to prison ministry resulted in doctoral studies focused on biblical storytelling in digital culture and to the "Breath of Fresh Air" project. The positive results of that project are continually reinforced by on-going work at the jail. They drive my advocacy of Circle of the Word behind locked doors.

2

Mass Incarceration, Restorative Justice, and Biblical Storytelling

MASS INCARCERATION

With well over two million adults locked up in jails and prisons, the United States holds an unfortunate world record. In 2007 a resource developed for local congregations reported, "The United States has 5% of the world's population and 25% of its prisoners."[1] "Mass incarceration" is the label given this relatively new phenomenon. Michelle Alexander brought this phenomena to light on the lecture circuit and in her landmark book *The New Jim Crow*, where she defines mass incarceration as "a tightly networked system of laws, policies, customs, and institutions that operate collectively to ensure the subordinate status of a group defined largely by race."[2] The results are chilling:

> The United States now has the highest rate of incarceration in the world. Dwarfing the rates of nearly every developed country, even surpassing those in highly repressive regimes like Russia, China, and Iran. In Germany, 93 people are in prison for every 100,000

1. Heavner, "Congregational Tool Box for Prison Ministry," 4.
2. Alexander, *The New Jim Crow*, 13.

adults and children. In the United States, the rate is roughly eight times that, or 750 per 100,000.[3]

Our status as the #1 incarceration nation is not because American citizens are more likely to be criminals than the citizens of other countries, nor even because this nation has more crime. Statistics about crime do not show a positive relationship between crime and incarceration rates. The source is a combination of factors: political expediency, economic entanglement, and the legacy of slavery that still haunts our country.

A major cause of our status as the preeminent incarceration nation is the so-called "War on Drugs." This war was declared by President Richard Nixon in the 1970s. It has been waged by every subsequent administration in spite of its dismal failure. According to an award-winning documentary film called "The House I Live In":

> For over 40 years, the War on Drugs has accounted for 45 million arrests, cost over $1 trillion, has made America the world's largest jailer and has damaged poor communities at home and abroad. Yet, drugs are cheaper, purer and more available today than ever.[4]

The only benefactors of this war have been those capitalizing on an ever-expanding prison industry. According to Bryan Stevenson in his book *Just Mercy*, "The privatization of prison health care, prison commerce, and a range of services has made mass incarceration a money-making windfall for a few and a costly nightmare for the rest of us."[5] Stevenson should know. As a lawyer and executive director of Equal Justice Initiative, he has been involved with litigation concerning death row inmates for thirty years.

High incarceration rates of young, poor, minority citizens—those who have flooded American jails and prisons in recent history—make a mockery of the term "justice" in the name "criminal justice system." As Alexander points out, "Sociologists have frequently observed that governments use punishment primarily as a tool of social control, and thus the extent or severity of punishment is often unrelated to actual crime patterns."[6] Common sense would treat substance abuse as a health issue, not a crime. Why is the use and sale of drugs such as tobacco and alcohol legal, while the use and sale of others is not? Why has the possession of one form of an

3. Ibid., 6.
4. Jarecki, *The House I Live In*.
5. Stevenson, *Just Mercy*, 17.
6. Alexander, *The New Jim Crow*, 7.

illegal drug (crack cocaine) been dealt with much more harshly than the possession of that same drug in another form (powder cocaine)? These are examples from just one area of injustice in the American criminal justice system.

High incarceration rates do not make American communities safer. The threat of incarceration does not effectively deter crime. Most people who "do time" return to their communities. Many returning citizens commit new crimes, inflicting further hurt on themselves and their communities. According to the Horizon Prison Initiative: "Upon release approximately 50% will reoffend and return to prison within three years."[7] This high recidivism rate suggests that current practices are not "correcting" behavior as one might think would be the case with the new "corrections" language of incarceration.

Incarceration increases obstacles to productive citizenship for returning citizens. These "collateral sanctions" impact housing, employment, and even voting. The experience of incarceration rarely addresses the factors that led people there; it frequently exacerbates them. People behind bars are more likely to learn how to be better criminals than how to be better citizens. In the words of Horizon staff, "Unless something is done to end this decades-old trend that weakens all facets of society, we will all continue to pay the price."

The conceptual framework for the American criminal justice system is retributive. It is a legacy of ancient Rome with its brutal slave law. The Dutch historian of law, Herman Bianchi, concluded: "It was precisely this retributive law that was taken over into highly punitive Western ways of criminal justice."[8] Operating with a retributive justice paradigm, society punishes individuals who do not conform to its laws. Punishment is meant first and foremost to uphold the power of the state by discouraging lawbreaking and encouraging law-abiding. It also serves to satisfy the desire for revenge by victims and their families. It often masquerades as justice.

In the past, punishment was primarily achieved through banishment from the community or physical harm (e.g., whipping, mutilation, hanging). Imprisonment as punishment is a relatively recent practice, replacing previous practices of physical harm, except in the case of capital crimes. Imprisonment as punishment involves captivity, isolation, and reduced

---

7. FAQ paper, Horizon Prison Initiative, 2014.

8. Allard and Northey, "The Rediscovery of Restorative Justice," 127.

rights. It is the keystone of the American criminal justice system and increasingly a millstone for healthy community.

According to a front page article published in the *New York Times* on July 5, 2016:

> There is a growing consensus that the criminal justice system has incarcerated too many Americans for too many years, with liberals and conservatives alike denouncing the economic and social costs of holding 2.2 million people in the nation's prisons and jails.[9]

Even those at the center of the criminal justice system are recognizing its deficiencies and are calling for change. Federal Judge Walter Rice, speaking from fifty years of experience in the criminal justice system, recently said, "Judges everywhere have recognized that the way our criminal system works is not very effective—we've got to start doing things differently."[10] He said that most judges know this, but some are in communities stuck in the old "lock 'em up and throw away the key" mentality where change is not possible.

Judge Rice advocates for communities to help people who want to help themselves. He contends that everyone deserves a second chance on the condition of having made a conscious decision to change his or her life. Judge Rice has been a leader in establishing "Reentry courts" in Montgomery County, Ohio. A reentry court is a specialized court for offenders who leave prison early and reenter society. Judge Rice gave three reasons to take a new approach: (1) it is the right thing to do, (2) our criminal justice budget here and everywhere "has gone through the roof," and (3) helping people help themselves is the best public safety measure.

Articulating the sense in which taking a new approach is the right thing to do, Bryan Stevenson writes:

> I've come to believe that the true measure of our commitment to justice, the character of our society, our commitment to the rule of law, fairness, and equality cannot be measured by how we treat the rich, the powerful, the privileged, and the respected among us. The true measure of our character is how we treat the poor, the disfavored, the accused, the incarcerated, and the condemned.[11]

9. Williams, "A '90s Legacy," A1, A11.

10. Walter H. Rice is a federal judge for the U.S. District Court serving on senior status. He spoke at the "Restoration, Recovery, and Re-Entry Conference" held at United Theological Seminary in Dayton, Ohio on October 11, 2014.

11. Stevenson, *Just Mercy*, 18.

These words echo the prophets of old and the teachings of the Nazarene, Jesus. They are not words spoken in a vacuum. There is a movement in American society toward a different approach than the retributive model of criminal justice: restorative justice.

RESTORATIVE JUSTICE

The advocacy and action of Judge Rice reflects the movement that has begun in this country toward an alternative to the retributive model of criminal justice. The approach this movement advocates is called "restorative justice." It has roots in Aboriginal traditions "that use the principles of healing and living in harmony with all beings and with nature as the basis for mending damaged personal and communal relationships."[12] It is also firmly grounded in biblical tradition. In his seminal work, *Changing Lenses,* Howard Zehr proposes restorative justice as a new paradigm for justice based on the biblical concepts of *shalom,* covenant, and righteousness.

These concepts were established in the Old Testament and further developed in the New Testament for a new context. They were not lost on the early church fathers. In 412 CE, Augustine invoked the concepts in a letter he wrote to Marcellinus, a judge appointed by Emperor Honorius. In the letter Augustine pleads with Marcellinus to refrain from maiming or executing members of the Donatist faction who had maimed, beaten, and killed members of Augustine's Catholic community:

> Fulfil, Christian judge, the duty of an affectionate father; let your indignation against their crimes be tempered by considerations of humanity; be not provoked by the atrocity of their sinful deeds to gratify the passion of revenge, but rather be moved by the wounds which these deeds have inflicted on their own souls to exercise a desire to heal them.[13]

Augustine counseled against retribution. He advocated restoration. The paradigm Zehr proposes is not really new.

In *Changing Lenses,* Zehr unpacks the three basic meanings of the Hebrew word *shalom*: physical well-being, right relationship, and integrity. Shalom is God's will for the world. According to Zehr: "Shalom defines how God intends things to be. God intends people to live in a condition of 'all rightness'

---

12. Umbreit and Armour, *Restorative Justice Dialogue,* 67.

13. Philip Schaff, *Confessions and Letters of St. Augustin.*

in the material world; in interpersonal, social and political relationships; and in personal character."[14] Zehr then presents covenant as "the basis and primary model" of biblical shalom. In the ancient near east a covenant was a binding agreement between two parties each of which had certain rights and responsibilities. The Israelites distinguished themselves from other peoples by applying the concept of covenant to their relationship with God. They believed God had initiated a covenant with them and repeatedly acted to restore right relationship with them, even though they regularly failed to uphold their commitments. God's salvation was delivered out of God's love, not because it was earned or deserved.

The discussion of covenant leads Zehr to the concept of justice which he describes as "a measuring stick to test for shalom."[15] An important characteristic of biblical justice is its holistic nature. It is the work of making things right, as exemplified over and over again by God with regard to re-establishing shalom. It is making things right again after the people have messed up.

Under the influence of Greco-Roman culture, the holistic concept of justice was bifurcated into "social" or "distributive" justice and "criminal" or "retributive" justice. Zehr explains the difference: "When we talk about wrongs having to do with the distribution of wealth and power, we call these questions of social justice. When we talk about wrongs legally defined as crimes we categorize this as the realm of retributive justice."[16] Political expediency has led to more action with regard to retributive than distributive justice. Thus, "Get tough on crime" has been much more successful in garnering votes than "Equal pay for equal work."

And yet, the holistic sense of justice characteristic of the biblical tradition persists in American thought and action. In the mid-nineteenth century Theodore Parker, a Unitarian minister, worked for the abolition of slavery. In a sermon entitled "Of Justice and the Conscience" he said: "I do not pretend to understand the moral universe, the arc is a long one, my eye reaches but little ways. I cannot calculate the curve and complete the figure by the experience of sight; I can divine it by conscience. But from what I see I am sure it bends towards justice."[17]

14. Howard Zehr, *Changing Lenses*, 132.

15. Ibid., 136.

16. Ibid., 1990, 137.

17. Parker, *Ten Sermons of Religion*.

A century later Martin Luther King, Jr. echoed Parker's sentiment in his famous statement: "The arc of the moral universe is long but it bends toward justice." Zehr calls for a paradigm of justice in American civil life consistent with the biblical understanding of justice advocated by Parker and King. He called it "covenant justice" in 1990.

As the conversation developed, by the turn of the millennium it had come to be called "restorative justice." Zehr defined the concept: "Restorative justice is a process to involve, to the extent possible, those who have a stake in a specific offense and to collectively identify and address harms, needs, and obligations, in order to heal and put things as right as possible."[18] Further testimony to this movement comes from Pierre Allard and Wayne Northey: "Over the last twenty-five years, there have been a number of initiatives in many countries challenging us to go beyond a retributive justice to a restorative justice. These initiatives have been emerging signs of hope calling for a radical reengagement of the Christian faith in criminal justice issues from a restorative justice perspective."[19] Restorative justice is not just an American movement, nor just a Christian movement. But it is a movement that can be empowered by a Christian perspective true to its biblical origins.[20]

The United Methodist Church shares this new paradigm of justice and has joined the restorative justice movement. Its "Social Principles" include a strong endorsement of foundational understandings and principles. The statement includes a succinct description of what restorative justice is and how it differs from retributive justice. That statement is quoted in its entirety here:

> In the love of Christ, who came to save those who are lost and vulnerable, we urge the creation of a genuinely new system for the care and restoration of victims, offenders, criminal justice officials, and the community as a whole. Restorative justice grows out of biblical authority, which emphasizes a right relationship with God, self, and community. When such relationships are violated or broken through crime, opportunities are created to make things right.
>
> Most criminal justice systems around the world are retributive. These retributive justice systems profess to hold the offender accountable to the state and use punishment as the equalizing

18. Zehr, *The Little Book of Restorative Justice*, 37.

19. Allard and Northey, "Rediscovery of Restorative Justice," 135.

20. For an excellent discussion of restorative justice from a Catholic perspective see Levad, *Redeeming a Prison Society*, 112–126.

tool for accountability. In contrast, restorative justice seeks to hold the offender accountable to the victimized person, and to the disrupted community. Through God's transforming power, restorative justice seeks to repair the damage, right the wrong, and bring healing to all involved, including the victim, the offender, the families, and the community. The Church is transformed when it responds to the claims of discipleship by becoming an agent of healing and systemic change.[21]

As is evident from this statement, the restorative justice movement in response to crime has both secular and spiritual dimensions. At the same time, it respects the principle of separation of church and state.[22] Circle of the Word positions itself in the context of the restorative justice movement. It seeks to address the spiritual dimensions of restorative justice. It also adapts for use a primary practice of restorative justice, the *peacemaking circle.*

Peacemaking circles are inspired by Native American talking circles. They structure a way for people to engage in conversation that allows each person an equal opportunity to speak without fear of interruption, and to listen without feeling pressure to respond. The form and the process create a safe, non-hierarchical environment for sharing ideas, perceptions, and feelings. Most of all, participants are encouraged and enabled to tell their personal stories. The circle is an egalitarian form, with all points in the circle being in equal relation to the center. No member of the circle is more or less valued than any other member. Each member of the circle has the opportunity to let his or her voice be heard. Expectations are clarified and agreed upon by all participants. Values of the peacemaking circle include respect, honesty, and patience.

Once a topic for conversation has been identified by the *circlekeeper,* a *talking piece* facilitates the circle process. This is an object that is passed from one person to another to indicate whose turn it is to speak. Only the person holding the talking piece speaks; all others listen. A person may choose to hold the talking piece in silence, or simply pass it on to the next person. The flow of a peacemaking circle is also clearly structured with well defined opening and closing segments. These may combine a regular ritual or ceremony with more varied activities.

21. "Social Principles: Political Community."
22. Specific examples are avoidance of proselytizing and voluntary programming.

Circle processes have been applied to many different contexts and purposes. The group, Women Writing for (a) Change, employs a circle structure that has empowered women to write since 1991.[23] In the late twentieth century, circle processes began to be used as an alternate way of sentencing in Canada. The practice became more widespread through the work of Kay Pranis, who served as the Restorative Justice Planner for the Minnesota Department of Corrections for nine years. Pranis developed training methods and resources that spread the practice in this country. It has been used extensively with youth gang members on Chicago's south side by Fr. Dave Kelly, Executive Director of Precious Blood Ministry of Reconciliation. Under his leadership, circle training has been established in Dayton, Ohio and is practiced in a number of settings including the Montgomery County Jail.

BIBLICAL STORYTELLING

Long before we had a book called a Bible read in silence and studied objectively as a source for theological doctrines, people gathered in small groups telling their stories of God and community. Relationship with God was personal, immediate, and grounded in family narrative that was both informative and enjoyable. This is the oral culture of Abraham and Sarah, the culture in which our faith tradition had its origins. It is the communication culture of many in today's prisons, where orality abounds.

When it comes to learning and telling God's stories by heart, God laid down the law. Deuteronomy 6:4–7 became the central confession of the people of Israel. It is named after its first word in Hebrew, *Shema*, which means "hear." The Shema calls us to intimate, covenantal relationship by having God's words in our hearts and reciting them to others. Sacred story is at the heart of faith formation.

A primary way of showing our love for God is to commit our time, energy and intellectual ability in learning God's stories by heart. This is not mere memorization. Memorization is an activity limited to the head. It is disconnected, surface knowledge of the story. It is only a first step on the way to a goal. The goal of biblical storytelling is internalization. Internalization is when the story becomes part of your story so that you tell it just like you would tell the story of your childhood or any familiar incident in your

---

23. For more information, visit www.womenwriting.org. Other uses of circle processes are listed in Pranis, *The Little Book of Circle Processes*, 17–18.

life. This kind of knowing the story takes time and patience. It is getting the stories of God into long-term memory.

How does this happen? What is the way to internalization of God's stories? Many persons think that they are not capable of learning stories by heart. But all humans, young and old, literate and illiterate, have great capacity for storing and accessing biblical stories in their long-term memory. Biblical storytelling workshops teach specific stories using pedagogical methods designed to maximize this capacity. A standard workshop has a four-part structure:

1. Learn the story—first its basics (setting, characters, plot), then specific words and phrases

2. Explore the story in its original context—how the story would have been understood by audiences to whom it was first told

3. Connect the story to contemporary life—relating dynamics of the story to one's own lived experience

4. Tell the story—communicating through voice and gesture

The design of a biblical storytelling workshop follows this structure in a linear fashion. In practice, however, the four elements weave in and out among each other as the workshop proceeds.

Teaching biblical stories using oral methods has the side benefit of assisting with the task of reading. Low literacy rates are the norm in a prison population. Incarcerated persons are typically more skilled at oral communication than literate. Oral learning methods include the most ancient form of education, technically called "chirping" but more descriptively called "repeat-after-me." Gestures and movements are repeated, as well as words, so that kinesthetic intelligence is brought into play along with verbal intelligence. This method works well for everyone and does not leave oral learners at a disadvantage. In fact, oral learners have an advantage over literate learners when it comes to biblical storytelling.

I initially designed Circle of the Word as a completely oral experience. I found, however, that most of those who attend are able, willing, and pleased with the opportunity to read aloud. Therefore, as Circle of the Word developed, I incorporated more reading into its design. I avoid pressuring anyone who cannot read to do so. I do not want to inject any source of shame into the Circle experience.

The story of Jesus and the children inspires the spirit of biblical story-telling workshops. A goal I often state is to "enjoy the story together." The purpose of the workshop time is not to learn something in the head that can then be recited as biblical "proof" of a particular idea. The purpose is to establish connection to the characters of God's story, especially to Jesus. The purpose is growth in relationship with God. It is the work of spiritual formation. The purpose is ultimately to receive the kingdom of God "as a little child" (Mark 10:15).

CIRCLE OF THE WORD

Mass incarceration in the United States raises significant issues and manifold needs. There is the need for political action to change laws with unjust and discriminatory sentencing and overly punitive measures for non-violent crimes. There is the need to curtail the privatization of prisons, where communities and companies profit by keeping people incarcerated. There is the need to transform public opinion about the purpose of imprisonment from punishment to whatever degree of reconciliation is possible. There is the need to address illiteracy, housing, family relations, substance abuse, emotional trauma, employment, domestic violence, and poverty.

Mass incarceration is a new form of disenfranchisement of African Americans, a new way in which racism has impacted public policy. The War on Drugs, privatization of the prison system, and location of prisons in rural white communities indicate the degree to which our criminal justice system serves as a vehicle for oppressive social injustice that dates back to slavery. Factoring in racial, economic, and educational inequities which drive the pipeline to prison for so many African American children, it is obvious that involvement with people caught up in the criminal justice system means involvement with issues of racial justice.

Issues and needs are obvious at the grass roots as well. A woman in the Grace Church neighborhood shared her concern for children who have nowhere to go when both parents are incarcerated. They are put in foster care, which may or may not provide good care. She told me that without her intervention this would have happened to her granddaughter. She envisioned a group home to care for these children. The neighborhood coordinator at the local public school knows from daily contact with students that "lots of them" have parents in jail or prison, now or in the past. Her estimate was one in four. The fact that several of the small group of children attending our church in recent years had parents in prison is a reflection of the difficult reality for many children in predominantly poor neighborhoods like the one surrounding Grace.

Whether national or local, these issues seem so big and the needs so pervasive that it is easy to feel helpless in the face of the behemoth of mass incarceration. Some may tackle the beast through expertise in social work, politics, or law. Those of us steeped in biblical tradition also have much to offer. Federal Judge Walter Rice emphasized that those who successfully re-entered the community following incarceration were those who were spiritually grounded. Geoffrey Canada, founder of the Harlem Children's Zone, specified the essential role of faith and hope in helping children raised in urban poverty beat the odds they face.

A poignant description of what happens to the spirit behind bars came from an inmate who participated in a Circle of the Word action research project. He said, "When incarcerated you are like a fatherless child looking for hope."[24] There is a need to develop practices that provide prisoners with the spiritual grounding to find light in their darkness and hope for their future. They need a breath of fresh air that will fill them with the Spirit of Life. This is the need addressed by Circle of the Word.

How can healthy spiritual formation be facilitated for people in jail or prison? Not all approaches are helpful. Mary Hallinan is a leader in the restorative justice movement in Dayton. She leads a peacemaking circle for women in jail that explores positive values and character traits. She observes the importance of the Bible to many of these incarcerated women: "They cling to it like a lifesaver." But she is also aware of the way in which the Bible is potentially harmful to them. The patriarchal bent of some approaches to Christianity and biblical literature can be counterproductive to healthy spiritual development for these women, many of whom have been abused by men.

Chaplain Willie Templeton described some approaches to ministry in the Montgomery County Jail as a hindrance rather than a help saying, "A lot of times the leaders of a Bible study or worship service can come off as self righteous or judgmental . . . and beat them over the head about their decision-making."[25] Other chaplains in correctional settings in other

24. Response to interview question about the impact of the project on people who are incarcerated, May 13, 2014.

25. Interview with Willie Templeton, June 18, 2014, Montgomery County Jail, Dayton, Ohio.

communities paint a similar picture. A new approach to engaging the scriptures is needed for women and men living behind bars.

All humans are in need of healing and liberation, supportive community, repentance, forgiveness, empowerment, and hope. People in detention settings have the time and in some cases the will to pursue fulfillment of these needs. As Chaplain Templeton comments, "You don't have to tell an inmate that they're wrong. They know they're wrong, they're in jail . . . Some folks come in and they're just ready to change."[26] The faith premise of Circle of the Word is that the Word of God may come like a breath of fresh air to fill spiritual needs of people in jail or prison through interactive engagement with biblical stories in a safe, small group context. Biblical storytelling enables "the Voice that began creation"[27] to give a voice to the voiceless.[28] Internalizing biblical scriptures to tell oneself and others connects people to God and to each other in a positive way. The Circle of the Word experience involves hearing, learning, telling, and creatively engaging stories from the biblical tradition as a means of spiritual empowerment.

26. Interview, June 18, 2014.

27. Line from a prayer song.

28. Ellison describes the lack of voice prevalent among those who do time in *Cut Dead But Sill Alive*. In *Hear Me, See Me*, Redmond and Bartlett describe the impact for incarcerated women of being given "the chance to be heard, really heard," 10.

3

A New Paradigm
of Biblical Engagement

BIBLICAL PERFORMANCE CRITICISM

FIFTEEN YEARS BEFORE HOWARD Zehr called for a paradigm shift with regard to crime and justice, Walter Wink perceived a similar need in the realm of biblical study.[1] He published a manifesto that began with the provocative statement, "Historical biblical criticism is bankrupt."[2] Expanding on the business metaphor, he explained that bankruptcy does not mean that the traditional method of biblical study developed in modernity is without value, but that, as Wink said, "it is no longer able to accomplish its avowed purpose for existence."[3] Circle of the Word shares what Wink articulated as the purpose for biblical study: "to interpret the Scriptures that the past becomes alive and illumines our present with new possibilities for personal and social transformation."[4] Wink's critique of the historical critical method as having "reduced the Bible to a dead letter"[5] echoes Martin

---

1. For a discussion of Howard Zehr's work, see the section on Restorative Justice in chapter 1.

2. Wink, *The Bible in Human Transformation*, 1.

3. Ibid., 1.

4. Ibid., 2.

5. Ibid., 4.

Luther and is shared by many today who desire on-going relevance of the biblical tradition.

Wink places responsibility for the bankruptcy of historical biblical criticism on "objectivism."[6] Objectivism is the attempt to study the Bible as an unbiased observer, free from any influence of emotion, ego involvement, or constraining context. It is an attempt doomed to failure that distorts reality by refusing to admit essential aspects of reality (such as emotion, vested interests, and social location). Objectivism plays out in many ways, for example, in ignoring the impact of gender, ethnicity, class, and sexual orientation on biblical interpretation. But first and foremost, it leads the interpreter to approach the Bible with "detached neutrality in matters of faith,"[7] which cuts against its original reason for being and trivializes the hermeneutical enterprise.

The heart of Wink's critique is the lack of what he calls, "participational involvement in the 'object' of research" with the result that "'truth' is reduced to facticity."[8] These shortcomings are avoided by a primary characteristic of biblical performance criticism: the practice of storytelling as a beginning, a means, and an end of research. According to Tom Boomershine, in storytelling "the meaning is only minimally connected with ideas or facts."[9] The meaning of a storytelling event is connected with experience.

Wink identifies two further signs of dysfunction stemming from objectivism which contribute to the need for a new paradigm of biblical study. First, there is its "uncontrolled technologism."[10] By this he means limiting study to those questions that can be addressed and measured by the techniques of high literate methodology. This is the issue Werner Kelber addresses in an interview for a documentary on biblical performance criticism: "As far as the minute understanding of biblical texts and excessive detail is concerned: that is a preoccupation once again of a type of scholarship which is totally literary, which operates with print documents and has lost touch with the oral dimension of our biblical manuscripts."[11] The

---

6. "Objectivism" is not to be confused with "objectivity" which Wink strongly endorses. Biblical study without any degree of objectivity, with its frequent partner anti-intellectualism, creates another set of distortions. But these are not typical of biblical engagement in the academic world which has so influenced mainstream Christianity.

7. Wink, *The Bible in Human Transformation*, 2.

8. Ibid.

9. Boomershine, *The Messiah of Peace*, 10.

10. Wink, *The Bible in Human Transformation*, 15.

11. Botha, *Orality, Print Culture and Biblical Interpretation*.

scholars of whom Kelber speaks probably were not in touch with the oral dimension of the manuscripts since the oral dimension is part of the new paradigm.

The other sign of dysfunction stemming from objectivism is the separation of research from "vital community." As Wink explains:

> Historical criticism sought to free itself from the community in order to pursue its work untrammeled by censorship and interference. With that hard-won freedom it also won isolation from any conceivable significance.[12]

Wink rests his case for the bankruptcy of traditional biblical criticism with the assertion that it developed and had purpose in an historical context which is no more. His conclusion for current times is dire: "In the present context it is, as now practiced, obsolete."[13] Wink did not advance a new paradigm. Insofar as he pointed in that direction—"Toward a New Paradigm"—he proposed a combination of Socratic question-and-answer method with Jungian depth psychology, as practiced by a colleague for many years. He advocated communal exegesis led by a biblical interpreter who could facilitate transformative interaction with the Bible.

Sharon Ringe and Tom Boomershine, both students of Wink, took his call for a new paradigm of biblical study seriously. In different ways they explored what it might be to interpret the scriptures in such a way that the past becomes alive and illumines our present with new possibilities for personal and social transformation. Ringe's roadmap for biblical interpretation, co-authored with Fred Tiffany, emphasizes the reality of subjectivity and the importance of describing context with regard to the researcher and the scriptures.

Ringe and Tiffany are forthright in approaching study from a faith perspective. They highlight the role of the faith community in research. The process of biblical study outlined in *Biblical Interpretation: A Roadmap* includes techniques of objective inquiry as a means, not an end: "The purpose is not simply to multiply information . . . The goal is rather that each participant's world be transformed through the encounter with the worlds of other interpreters, as they come into dialogue with the biblical text."[14]

---

12. Wink, *The Bible in Human Transformation*, 10–11.

13. Ibid., 11.

14. Tiffany and Ringe, *Biblical Interpretation*, 46–47.

The call sounds again to help people engage with the Bible in order to make a concrete, positive difference in their lives.

Through his study of theatrical performance, experience of African American preaching, experimentation with biblical storytelling, and attention to new insights of communication theory and orality studies, Boomershine pushed the paradigm shift much further. Strongly influenced by the work of the Jesuit scholar, Walter Ong, Boomershine recognized the significance of major changes in modes of communication for studying and interpreting the Bible. He clarified that the heart of the need for a new paradigm of biblical study is the recognition that the Bible is not, as assumed by practitioners of the historical critical method, a static written document meant to be read in silence by individual readers. It is rather a collection of recordings of dynamic oral presentations and scripts meant to aid the memory of oral performers addressing communal audiences.

Dennis Dewey, reflecting on his vocation as a biblical storyteller, provides a helpful metaphor: "The written/printed text, as we have it in the Bible is a transcript of a performance, the fossil record of a lively storytelling tradition."[15] Even when the tradition does point to an original document, as with the letters of Paul, the delivery of these letters—their publication—was oral and lively. The radical implication for biblical scholarship is the need for the interpreter to internalize the composition[16] and experience it with an audience. That is, in this paradigm the composition is learned "by heart" in accordance with what we know about how it might have been heard, understood, and experienced in its original context.

This is achieved, insofar as it can be achieved, by taking advantage of knowledge coming from a variety of academic disciplines, by the process of internalizing itself, by telling it to an audience, and by engaging that audience in responding to the telling. Boomershine promoted the practice of communal learning by developing a workshop approach to biblical engagement in which participants hear the story told, learn about how it was understood in its original context, explore its connections for their lives, and experience telling it to another person. These workshops combine many of the components found wanting by Wink in historical biblical study.

15. Dewey, "Performing the Living Word," 148.

16. Rather than using a metaphor reflecting manuscript or print culture, what previously was referred to as "scripture" or "text" will here be designated by "composition" (from the world of music). "Composer" will be used instead of "author," and "audience" will replace "reader." In addition there is the storyteller or performer who delivers the composition in the first place.

Boomershine co-founded the Network of Biblical Storytellers (NBS) with Adam Bartholomew "to encourage everyone to learn and tell biblical stories."[17] At the academic level, Boomershine started a section in the Society of Biblical Literature: The Bible in Ancient and Modern Media (fondly nicknamed BAMM). In the late 1980s he wrote *Story Journey: An Invitation to the Gospel as Storytelling* to introduce the new paradigm to popular audiences through discussion of its basic premises and processes. He applied the paradigm to ten Gospel stories. His promise that biblical storytelling will be a source of new life reinvests biblical study with the purpose for which it legitimately exists. Many have born witness to the fulfillment of this promise.

In the thirty years since *Story Journey* was published, the movement toward a new paradigm of biblical study has grown in scale, energy, and influence. For the past ten years "scholarly storytellers and storytelling scholars" have studied scripture together at the annual NBS Seminar under the leadership of Phil Ruge-Jones. The work which BAMM initiated has generated over twenty groups in the Society of Biblical Literature. David Rhoads, a driving force in developing and promoting the new paradigm, named it "Biblical Performance Criticism." Rhoads is editor of an academic book series devoted to this emerging discipline. The series was initiated with the 2009 publication of *The Bible in Ancient and Modern Media: Story and Performance*, edited by Holly Hearon and Phil Ruge-Jones.

The paradigm shift is revealed in Rhoads' answer to the question "What Is Performance Criticism?": "Biblical performance is not one more methodology added on to other methodologies. Rather, it is a paradigm shift from print medium to oral medium that has implications for the entire enterprise of New Testament studies."[18] On the surface, the shift seems simple enough. It is to understand the original character of what we call the Bible as an oral/aural event involving a performer and an audience in the context of a communication culture that pre-dates print culture. But biblical scholarship has been wedded to print culture for five centuries. Its practitioners now wear high-literate lenses.[19] The language of biblical study

17. Mission statement of NBS. For more information, visit www.nbsint.org.

18. Rhoads, "What is Performance Criticism?" 88. Rhoads focuses on the New Testament; the paradigm shift is equally relevant for Old Testament work as demonstrated by scholars such as David Carr, Marti Steussy and Norman Gottwald.

19. The fact that human culture has experienced another communication revolution and is now dominated by digital systems in some ways complicates the problem, but in other ways highlights it. Digital communication has more in common with oral

is the language of fixed marks on a surface: scripture, text, book, author, reader.

The shift is not so simple after all. It involves conceiving the Bible as a collection of compositions, like musical scores. It means understanding that these compositions point to original events, not to an original document. These events were dynamic, flexible, vital, participatory, engaging, transforming, empowering, emotional, communal, and temporal. The shift is from dead letters to experiential knowledge.

A primary consequence in the paradigm shift is awareness of the importance of sound. According to Boomershine: "The implication of the emerging picture of the communication culture of the ancient world is that the accurate exegesis of the meaning of these compositions in their original context requires a methodology that is congruent with the character of the manuscripts as a medium for the recording of sounds in performance."[20] This means paying attention to the dynamics of vocal quality and inflection including volume, pitch, pace, pronunciation, and pauses.[21]

In his commentary on the passion, death and resurrection of Jesus according to Mark, Boomershine draws on the extensive work of Margaret Lee and Bernard Brandon Scott to explain these dynamics: "The grammarians and rhetoricians of ancient Greek consistently describe the "colon" and the "period" as the basic units of sound in Greek oratory, drama, and poetry. The colon and the period were breath units, the colon being the words that can comfortably be said in one breath and the period as a combination of cola that build to a climax."[22] Once again there is a reminder of the preeminence of breath in communication of the faith tradition.

Not only sounds must be taken into consideration in biblical performance criticism, also physicality and presence. The story is embodied by a living person who gestures, uses facial expressions, and moves. As Whitney Shiner has made clear, in the cultures of the Ancient Near East words and gestures were not "divorced from each other" as they are in the print-oriented cultures of modernity.[23] Plato observed, "Some of us make gestures that are invariably in harmony with our words, but some of us

communication than literate. It is, as Walter Ong explains in *Orality and Literacy*, a kind of "secondary orality," 135.

20. Boomershine, *The Messiah of Peace*, 5.

21. Rhoads, "Performance Events in Early Christianity," 171.

22. Boomershine, *The Messiah of Peace*, 6.

23. Shiner, *Proclaiming the Gospel*, 127.

fail."[24] Gestures were taken seriously as an integral component of effective oral communication.

The analysis of gesture and movement for performing scriptures is an important part of biblical performance criticism. The study of ancient rhetorical gestures informs decisions about gestures in biblical speeches. For example, exaggerated gestures developed both to demonstrate skill in communication and to deal with the pragmatic problem of being heard when addressing a large and sometimes noisy crowd. The exaggerated gesture style that developed may well have transferred to performance of speeches before small groups as well.[25]

Besides rhetorical gestures, the other main type of gesture and movement used in the ancient world was imitative—the kind of gestures and movements employed by actors to imitate the voice and action of characters in their dramas. Storytelling combined both the rhetorical type (especially for speeches) and the imitative type (for action). Probably a continuum existed between those who favored rhetorical gesturing and those who favored mimetic gestures. According to Shiner. "Storytelling, or the performance of narrative, falls somewhere between these two styles, more imitative than orators but with more restrained action than the comic stage or the dance."[26] Awareness of this range of performance style informs contemporary interpretation.

Rhoads defines performance broadly: "any oral telling/retelling of a brief or lengthy tradition—from saying to gospel—in a formal or informal context of a gathered community by trained or untrained performers—on the assumption that every telling was a lively recounting of that tradition."[27] Performance involves complex factors of sound and physical presence. The task of understanding, interpreting and preserving the original meaning of written compositions is hard enough. When all we have left is a handful of scripts, it seems impossible to understand, interpret, and preserve the original meaning of a performance. One might wonder, why even try? A voice issues an ancient challenge: "Mortal, can these bones live?" (Ezek 37:3).

Rhoads calls the community of biblical scholarship to rise to the occasion and accept the challenge. It is a call for scholars and practitioners from diverse fields, drawing on approaches to biblical study that are traditional,

---

24. Ibid., quoting Plato, 127.

25. Ibid., 128.

26. Ibid., 135.

27. Rhoads, "Performance Criticism."

as well as those more recently developed.[28] His comprehensive explication of biblical performance criticism, published in the *Biblical Theology Bulletin* and available online, describes the nature of the challenge, lists the many and varied resources prepared to address it, and identifies enough investigative questions to keep the community working for many years.

The work has begun in earnest. While at an early stage, it is bearing fruit in numerous academic articles, books, teaching, and digital works reflecting the wide-ranging topics involved. The writing, telling, and digital production generated so far under the umbrella of biblical performance criticism is solid groundwork for biblical interpretation in digital culture.[29] Anyone who wishes to engage biblical performance criticism in the service of interpreting specific compositions can draw on this body of work for support and guidance.

It is also the case that at this early stage of the paradigm shift in biblical hermeneutics there are few examples of performance critical commentary of specific stories. There are no "how to" textbooks for seminary students. Most interpreters are still wearing the old lenses of the dominant paradigm, even when they are aware of the emerging one. The remainder of this chapter will attempt to lay out specifics for applying performance criticism to biblical stories. The number of variables involved are daunting and the limitations of describing a live performance in print are significant. Nevertheless, one can prophecy to the bones as commanded and then listen for the rattling to begin.

APPLYING THE PARADIGM: EXPERIENTIAL EXEGESIS

"Experiential exegesis" is the effort to explicate the original meaning of a specific segment of the biblical tradition as groundwork for a faithful telling.[30] The effort is at the same time objective and subjective. The value of

---

28. David Rhoads describes the possible contributions through each of the following list of methodological approaches: historical, form, genre, narrative, reader-response, rhetorical, textual, orality, social-science, linguistic, and ideological criticism; speech-act theory; translation, theater, and oral interpretation studies. See Part II of his essay in *Biblical Theology Bulletin* 36.

29. Wipf and Stock publishes a series devoted to performance criticism. Peter Perry and Jeanette Mathews administer a website dedicated to biblical performance criticism: www.biblicalperformancecriticism.org.

30. Boomershine first used this term in his courses on "Christianity & Communications in Contemporary Culture" at United Theological Seminary, 2004–2006.

exegesis is its respect for tradition by letting tradition speak for itself, and listening to what it has to say as objectively as possible in its original context, while being fully aware that pure objectivity is neither possible nor desirable. The value of experiential exegesis is its respect for tradition by participating in it, being impacted by it, and expecting that others will as well.

Furthermore, experiential exegesis names the kind of meaning that is the ultimate goal of biblical explication in the new paradigm: experiential. This is in contrast to the kind of meaning that developed in the communication culture of silent print following the invention of the printing press. Hans Frei called that kind "meaning as reference." It includes "ostensive reference" (the Bible as a source of historical information) and "ideal reference" (the Bible as a source of theological ideas).[31]

In other words, in the culture of silent print what made the Bible meaningful was its function as a reference book for historical and theological knowledge. It was valued as a sourcebook of "true" facts about history and "true" ideas about God. This contrasts with what was meaningful in the oral culture of antiquity. There, as Rhoads explains: "Meaning is in the whole event at the site of performance—sounds, sights, storytelling/speech, audience reaction, shared cultural beliefs and values, social location, and historical circumstances."[32] In digital culture referential meaning is important, but has lost determinative power. Authentic experience that evokes emotion, inspires action, motivates change, and produces hope carries the power in today's world.

The experiential exegesis used for Circle of the Word is organized around four basic elements: telling, story, storyteller, and audience. First, there is the event itself, unique in every instance. Under the literate paradigm this event would be called a "reading." The current trend in performance criticism is to call it a "performance" or a "composition-in-performance."[33] I will opt for the language of storytelling and refer to the event as a *telling*. In this book descriptions of the telling refer to contemporary events, whereas the other elements explore matters related to the original context.

Second, *story* will be used to designate the object of study. The story is that which is communicated from the faith tradition, referred to above as "a specific segment of the biblical tradition." In the documentary paradigm

---

31. Frei, *Eclipse of Biblical Narrative*, 86–104.

32. Rhoads, "Performance Criticism Part I," 126.

33. Ibid., 127.

this is called the "text" or "pericope." Both of these words are too wedded to literacy for use in performance criticism. Other options that have surfaced in the previous discussion of performance criticism are "tradition" and "composition." Each of these convey relevant aspects of meaning, but at the same time are too multivalent. I opt for the simplicity of "story" with its grounding in oral practice. Typically, "story" refers to a narrative with a setting, characters, and plot sequence. Biblical tradition includes laws, poetry, prophecies, and letters. Even these, however, can be understood as story, or at least as residing within a story.

Third, there is the *storyteller* who embodies the story. The storyteller literally gives the story breath so that it can stand on its feet and live. Storyteller refers both to those who told the story long ago and to those who tell it today. This book uses storyteller rather than performer because storyteller connotes more personal interaction with the story and with the audience. It is also less allied with drama, which is a significantly different art form than storytelling.

Audience is the fourth basic element. Audience refers to those who listen to the storyteller tell the story. Audience is implicitly, though not necessarily, plural. This is in keeping with the original character of the story experience. The audience is not assumed to be passively receptive, nor silent in their listening. They may laugh or grumble; they may express through verbal or non-verbal communication their pleasure, displeasure, engagement, or disengagement with the story. The audience may be given a way to participate in the storytelling event in some intentional manner—like a sung or spoken phrase, a movement, or a gesture. With an effective telling audience members will make connections with the story. They will identify with characters, experience associations with various aspects of the story, and be impacted by its dynamics.

Experiential exegesis is an attempt to listen to the story in its original context—that is, to understand how it was heard and experienced by its first audiences. It also considers the range of connections and responses of current audiences. For purposes of Circle of the Word there are two goals of the analysis. The first is to re-create a meaningful resemblance of the original performance experience for a contemporary audience. The second is to facilitate a small group engagement with the story for the sake of spiritual empowerment.

Aspects of this approach use standard exegetical methods drawing on the expertise of scholars as conveyed in biblical commentaries and reference tools. However, these methods are used in service of a performance critical study of the story grounded in its internalization and performance. That is, understanding develops in the process of learning the story by heart and telling it to an audience. Information and insights from those working in fields relevant to biblical performance criticism also contribute to the analysis.

The dynamic relationship between the four basic elements of experiential exegesis is apparent even in the process of naming them. They impact one another. To talk about one is to talk about the others. Nevertheless, different questions can be asked of each. In the discussion that follows, details for doing experiential exegesis are formed as questions and grouped in the four categories of telling, story, storyteller, and audience. The following list of questions is not all-inclusive, but establishes a manageable scope for Circle of the Word.

Telling

1. In what *space* will the telling occur? The physical venue for the telling makes a difference. Factors to consider are size, seating configuration, the presence or absence of a raised stage, acoustics/amplification, and the type of space (for example: park, tent, church, nursing home, jail).

2. What is the *occasion* for the telling? Occasion, like space, influences interpretive decisions with regard to language, voice, movement, and interaction with the audience.

3. Who is the *contemporary audience*? Do a majority of those in the audience share any common characteristics?

Story

1. What is the *narrative context* of the story? What is its larger story? What immediately precedes it? What follows it?

2. What *words* will be used to convey the story? Our modern standard translations were developed under the old paradigm, assuming that the recipients were silent readers. Examples include: (a) changing a word to its synonym to avoid repetition and thereby losing the storytelling benefits associated with verbal threads; (b) changing verbs in

historical present tense to past tense and thereby losing the sense of immediacy created by the historical present tense;[34] (c) inserting the identification of a speaker (e.g., "he said") in the middle of a quote instead of preceding it. As David Rhoads and others have pointed out, a "translation for performance" is sorely needed. There are also instances when standard translations use words that are not dynamic equivalents to the original words and distort their original meaning, or may be misunderstood in harmful ways by contemporary audiences.[35]

3. What is the *setting* of the story? What pointers to time and place are in the story? If none are given, can the setting be determined?

4. Who are the *characters*, both those directly involved in the story ("on-stage") and those who are referenced ("off stage")? What, if any, description is given of the characters and what is the perspective of the description? Is it an inside view about emotion, knowledge, or state of mind? Or is it a more objective description from an observer's perspective?

5. What concrete *objects* (both animate and inanimate) are present in the story—things, plants, animals?

6. Are there any specific, named *concepts* present in the story?

7. What is the *plot* of the story, the sequence of action and dialogue? Are there elements of surprise or conflict?

8. Are there *verbal threads* in the story? Verbal threads are repeated words or phrases. The repetition may be within the story itself, within its story context as preserved in the canonical book, or within the whole of the biblical tradition. Verbal threads aid memory, provide structure, and enhance meaning.

9. What is the *structure* of the story? What are the breath units (phrases and sentences),[36] the episodes (a cohesive short segment usually consisting of two to three sentences),[37] the parts (logical divisions of the

34. According to Richard Nordquist, "In rhetoric, the use of the present tense to report on events from the past is called *translatio temporum* ('transfer of times')."

35. Examples are the use of "Jews," especially in the Gospel of John, and the exclusive use of male pronouns in reference to God.

36. The technical terms from ancient Greek are "cola" and "period." See the discussion of basic sound groups in Lee and Scott, *Sound Mapping the New Testament*, 108–111.

37. Boomershine identifies the episode as a storytelling unit based on his analysis of the original Greek. See Boomershine, *Story Journey*, 24–28.

story with multiple episodes in each part), the sections (for long narratives such as the passion, death and resurrection story of Jesus)?

10. What are the *norms of judgment* present in the story? Norms of judgment are: "criteria of good and bad, right and wrong, that provide the basis for the storyteller's implicit appeals to the listeners."[38] Norms of judgment impact the attitude of the storyteller toward the story's various characters and their behavior. They are conveyed through tone of voice, facial expression, and gesture.

Storyteller

1. Experiential exegesis identifies the storyteller's flexible *identity*. At each point in the story, who is the storyteller? The identity of the storyteller is a dimension of the difference between drama and storytelling. In drama, actors fully embody their character, usually only one character in the drama. Storytellers, however, are always, first and foremost, themselves. Only secondarily does the storyteller take on the persona of a character. Furthermore, the storyteller presents all the characters in the story, not just one. In any given telling, at various points the storyteller is the narrator as well as the various characters. Phil Ruge-Jones observes, "While a storyteller has options about when to portray a character and when not to, he or she must take on the persona of a character when that character speaks."[39]

2. Are there any *narrative comments* in the story? These aside comments occur when the storyteller intervenes in the storyline to speak directly to the audience. The purpose of a narrative comment is to give information that the narrator thinks the audience needs in order to understand the story.[40] Narrative comments are signaled with tone of voice and eye contact. They may be accompanied by a change in body position (moving closer to the audience), gesture (a hand at the side of the mouth), or facial expression (for example, a knowing wink or a look of dismay).

---

38. Ibid., 75.
39. Ruge-Jones, "Mentored into Steadfast Love," 4.
40. Boomershine, *Story Journey*, 75.

3. How can the sounds of the story be transcribed in a *sound map*[41] to reflect how the storyteller has vocalized it with regard to tempo, pacing, and pitch? In a script, new sentences begin on the left margin. Sentences often consist of multiple lines; those following the first line are indented. Each line is said in one breath, which automatically creates a brief pause. If there are too many words in a line for it to fit on the page, the line continues below with a double indent. Lines that are long necessarily go fast in order to get through them in one breath; lines that are short are said slowly and generally with more emphasis. Commas indicate a slight pause or breath. Semi-colons or dashes indicate a slightly longer pause. With a comma, the voice continues at the same pitch; with a semi-colon, the pitch usually drops lower. A period indicates both a longer pause than a semi-colon and a definitive drop in the voice. Episodes of the story are delineated by a double space. At the end of an episode, the voice drops and a substantial pause is given. During a telling, this pause allows time for the audience to form mental images of what just transpired in the story. A lengthy pause enables time for reflection. For the storyteller, this is a time to focus on the next part of the story.

4. What is the *volume* and *tone* with which the storyteller delivers the story? Volume and tone are factors governed by stage directions in the story itself (e.g., "he cried out in a loud voice"), knowledge of the norms of judgment of the original storyteller and audience, and emotions either stated directly by the story or inferred from its plot.

5. What *gestures, facial expressions,* and *postures* might the storyteller employ during the course of the telling?

6. Experiential exegesis describes *movements* that the storyteller might have made as suggested, or in some cases directed, by the story. Will the storyteller move from place to place during the course of the telling? If so, what is the blocking?

7. An embodied storytelling event necessitates the *placement* of various narrative components. What placement of characters, places, or things might the storyteller have made to enhance visualization of the story?

8. What *mnemonic devices* are present in the story that can assist with its internalization and telling?

41. For a description of sound mapping, see Lee and Scott, *Sound Mapping*, 167–168.

Audience

1. Who were the people in the *original audience* of the story and what was their context?

2. What were the *emotional appeals* of the story? These would include elements of humor, pathos, delight, remorse, etc.

3. With regard to the story's characters, what are the *dynamics of distance*? According to Boomershine: "A primary factor in human relationships is emotional distance, which can range from intimacy and identification to hostility and alienation."[42] Dynamics of distance have to do with the emotional relationships between the characters embodied by the storyteller and the audience. A good story is characterized by fluctuating dynamics of distance.

4. Just as the storyteller has a flexible *identity*, so does the audience. There is no fourth wall in storytelling.[43] Experiential exegesis describes when the audience is being addressed as a character in the story. This phenomenon is named "audience address" by Tom Boomershine.[44] Experiential exegesis asks if there is a point in the telling when the audience is addressed as a character in the story. If so, people in the audience are invited to hear the words of the storyteller as being spoken directly to them. Ruge-Jones observes: "Those hearing the text performed are drawn into the story and become characters addressed within the story world."[45] Audience address is responsible for much of the transformative potential in biblical storytelling.

5. What are the *experiential connections* that the original audience and storyteller were invited to make with this story? This task should be approached with humility, for in many cases the best that can be done in answering this question is an informed guess.

6. What, then, is the intended *impact* of the story on the audience? Impact has to do with the thoughts, feelings and/or actions evoked in

---

42. Boomershine, *Story Journey*, 75.

43. The fourth wall is often a norm in drama. It is an imaginary wall between the audience and the actors. One of the significant differences between drama and storytelling is the absence of the fourth wall in storytelling.

44. Boomershine, "Audience Address and Purpose," 124–25.

45. Ruge-Jones, "Mentored into Steadfast Love."

response to encounter with the story. What did the story invite the audience to think, feel, or do?

7. In relation to the contemporary audience, what *connections, associations, and responses* are members of the audience likely to have? Each story will have a variety of possible hooks which draw people into involvement, and thereby into the possibility of being impacted by the story. This discussion may include examples from feedback of actual tellings.

Circle of the Word uses performance criticism/experiential exegesis in three ways. First of all, it is used in preparation for telling the stories. Secondly, key activities in a typical Circle draw heavily from the fruit of experiential exegesis. And thirdly, in the following sections it will be used to explicate the stories which support the guiding metaphor of this book and grounds it in biblical tradition. The story from the Old Testament is named "Dry Bones" (Ezek 37:1–14); the story from the New Testament is "Behind Locked Doors" (John 20:19–23).

4

Experiential Exegesis in Practice

THE PURPOSE OF THIS chapter is to provide specific examples of experiential exegesis that can serve as a model for the exegetical preparation of a story for Circle of the Word. The two stories chosen for this model have been foundational for this work. The word for "breath" in Hebrew, the original language of most of the Old Testament, is *ruach*. The word for "breath" in Greek, the original language of the New Testament, is *pneuma*. Both *ruach* and *pneuma* are used to convey a range of meanings—not only "breath," but also "wind" and "spirit." These terms figure prominently in the story of Ezekiel and the valley of dry bones (Ezekiel 37:1–14) and in the story of the resurrected Jesus appearing to his disciples behind locked doors (John 20:19–23).

Dry Bones and Behind Locked Doors are biblical stories that reflect both the experiences and the needs of people who are incarcerated: the experience of grievous loss, the quest for hope, and the promise of spiritual empowerment. A personal story told by Chaplain Templeton at a training meeting for jail volunteers echoes these dynamics:

> The young lady was convicted of killing her grandmother. She asked me if her life was over. I shared with her that although she had to give an account of her actions by going to prison, her life was not over. I explained to her that there were a lot of things she could do while in prison to help other young women who had addiction issues. She could get her education. She could take part in programs. Most of all she could give her life to Christ, and allow Him to shine through her as a shining example of what God can

do—no matter her situation. As I think back on that day, she was
hurting because she was high on drugs when she did this. Now she
was sober and trying to make sense out of all that had happened.

For this young woman, life as she knew it was gone. Could there be a breath
of fresh air in this situation? A source of hope for her future is present in
both Ezekiel and John.

Under King David the Israelite tribal confederacy united to become
a nation state. Soon after David's son Solomon died (922 BCE) the nation divided into northern and southern kingdoms: Israel and Judah. Two
hundred years later the northern kingdom fell to the Assyrians. Then in
587 BCE General Nebuzaradan, commander of Nebuchadnezzar's army,
delivered the deathblow to national identity when he torched Jerusalem
and the Temple and appropriated the southern kingdom for the Babylonian
empire. When the smoke cleared, in the words of John Bright, "the land
had been completely wrecked, its cities destroyed, its economy ruined, its
leading citizens killed or deported."[1] The prophet Ezekiel was among those
deported.

Just as Chaplain Templeton was called to minister to an imprisoned
young woman asking "Is my life over?" so also Ezekiel was called to speak
prophetic words to his captive people. The book of Ezekiel records the visions and words that explain how their present predicament is an account-
ing for breaking God's Law. Beyond judgment, Ezekiel's visions and words
promise new life. In the valley of dry bones, God asks Ezekiel the question
on the minds of the people, "Mortal, can these bones live?" (Ezek. 37:3a).
Obeying God's command, Ezekiel exhorts the people to trust the presence
and power of God, whatever their circumstance.

Six hundred years later, John expresses a similar sentiment through
the story of Jesus' appearance to his disciples on the evening of his resurrection. They are gathered behind locked doors in fear and defeat following
the brutal execution of their leader. Suddenly Jesus appears in their midst.
He greets them with peace, shows them evidence that it is really him, and
breathes on them so that they might receive God's spirit. He commissions
and empowers them for new purpose and new life, giving them reason to
hope.

Jesus' words spoke not only to the disciples of his day, but also to
those on the other side of the Roman-Judean war in the wake of which
John wrote his Gospel. Once again the holy city of the Judeans had been

1. Bright, *A History of Israel*, 331.

decimated. Once again the Temple destroyed, the walls leveled, the people killed, enslaved, and deported—their way of life gone. A breath of fresh air was needed in 587 BCE, in 33 CE at the time of Jesus' death, and again at the end of the first century in the aftermath of the Roman-Judean war. It is needed today in American jails and prisons. Circle of the Word may be an occasion for such a breath.

DRY BONES (EZEKIEL 37:1–14)

The Story

> The hand of the LORD came upon me
>> and brought me out by the spirit of the LORD
>> and set me down in the middle of a valley.
> It was full of bones.
>
> The spirit led me all around them.
> There were very many lying in the valley.
> And they were very dry.
>
> The LORD said to me, "Mortal, can these bones live?"
> I answered, "O Lord GOD, you know."

≈

> Then the Lord GOD said to me, "Prophesy to these bones, and say to
>> them:
>> O dry bones, hear the word of the LORD: Thus says the Lord GOD to
>>> these bones:
> I will cause breath to enter you, and you shall live.
> I will lay sinews on you, and will cause flesh to come upon you, and cover
>> you with skin,
>> and put breath in you, and you shall live, and you shall know that I
>>> am the LORD."
>
> So I prophesied as I had been commanded.
> And as I prophesied, suddenly there was a noise, a rattling, and the bones
>> came together,
>> bone to its bone.

45

I looked, and there were sinews on them, and flesh had come upon them,
and skin had covered them, but there was no breath in them.

～

Then the Lord GOD said to me,
"Prophesy to the breath; prophesy, mortal, and say to the breath:
Thus says the Lord GOD:
Come from the four winds, O breath, and breathe upon these slain,
that they may live."
I prophesied as the Lord GOD commanded me,
and the breath came into them,
and they lived,
and stood on their feet, a vast multitude.

～

Then the Lord GOD said to me, "Mortal, these bones are the whole house
of Israel.
They say, 'Our bones are dried up, and our hope is lost; we are cut off
completely.'

Therefore prophesy, and say to them, Thus says the Lord GOD:
I am going to open your graves, and bring you up from your graves, O my
people,
and I will bring you back to the land of Israel.
And you shall know that I am the LORD, when I open your graves,
and bring you up from your graves, O my people.

I will put my spirit within you, and you shall live, and I will place you on
your own soil.
Then you shall know that I, the Lord, have spoken and will act," says the
LORD.

～

The story of Dry Bones comes toward the end of Ezekiel. For most of the
epic, the prophet has spelled out in painful detail all the shortcomings of his
people and the reasons for their defeat and captivity. Having made God's
judgment clear, he then tells how God will act for God's own sake to save

the people and bring them out of captivity. This prophecy culminates with the image of "ruined towns filled with flocks of people" (Ezek. 36:38), setting the stage for the story of Dry Bones.

The above sound map for telling the story follows the New Revised Standard Version (NRSV) translation. An exception is language for God. Referents to God have been changed to neutralize gender. The pronoun "he" is in the first instance eliminated and in subsequent occurrences replaced by whatever word most recently has been used in reference: "spirit," "Lord," or "Lord God." God is neither male nor female but when God is constantly referenced as male the image of God one develops is male. Male imagery for God grew out of a patriarchal social structure and has reinforced the same cultural patterns for millennia. On the assumption that patriarchy oppresses both men and women, and that it is time to develop new social patterns, one strategy for change is to alter language for God. This is particularly important when a biblical story is going to be internalized and told by heart.

The story divides rather neatly into four parts. It begins with an action phrase: "The hand of the Lord came upon me." Part one then establishes the setting, introduces the characters and significant objects in the story, and sets up the plot. The plot is a series of three commands to prophesy. There is one command for each of the subsequent three parts, all of which begin with the same phrase: "Then the Lord God said to me . . ." In parts two and three the command to prophesy constitutes the first episode, while the second episode reports the actual prophecy with its result. In part four, all three episodes relate God's speech. There is no report of Ezekiel's response. However, the audience can safely assume he obeyed the task he was given since he has been obedient throughout the epic. The story concludes with promises of intimate relationship with God, new life, and return to the homeland.

The opening verses of the Ezekiel epic establish a beginning date as the fifth year of the Babylonian exile (593 BCE) and locate it in Mesopotamia. This is the general setting for the Dry Bones story. There are a number of subsequent time markers, the closest preceding the Dry Bones story is news of the fall of Jerusalem. This news came to Ezekiel "in the twelfth year of our exile, in the tenth month, on the fifth day of the month" which would be January 19, 585 BCE (Ezek 33:21).

Ezekiel was a priest who lived in Jerusalem until its first defeat by Nebuchadnezzar. His wife died, and he was deported to Babylon along with other leaders. There he received visions and messages from God to communicate to his exiled people. Cut off from the temple, he had no place to function as a priest. He was given a new role: prophet. In his description of ancient prophets, Joseph Blenkinsopp speaks from the perspective of the performance criticism paradigm: "The people we call prophets were—to risk a generalization—public orators and emotional preachers rather than authors. They did not set out to write a book but to persuade by the spoken word."[2]

Ezekiel recounts visions and messages in an objective narrative style with little autobiographical detail. One exception occurs in the account of his wife's death. We learn that Ezekiel had a wife who was "the delight of [his] eyes" (Ezek 24:16). But when she dies, the Lord instructs Ezekiel to refrain from normal lamentation practices and keep his feelings to himself: "Sigh, but not aloud; make no mourning for the dead" (Ezek 24:17). Similar instructions are given to the people in preparation for their impending disaster and monumental loss.

The Dry Bones story takes place in a broad, unnamed valley. Scholars have speculated about the specific location of this valley, hypothesizing that it was the site of a great battle in which many Israelite warriors were killed. While this is plausible, the story does not identify its location historically or geographically. The valley functions imaginatively as a place to which Ezekiel was transported by the Spirit of God. A literal location does not matter. What does matter are the bones. This valley is a place of death, desolation, and despair.

The story has two main characters who are introduced in the opening line. "The hand of the LORD came upon me" is Ezekiel's characteristic way of describing the beginning of a vision. The story is told in first person from Ezekiel's point of view. The Lord is the other main character, embodied with a "hand" that comes upon Ezekiel and leads him all around the valley. Yet the Lord is also the Spirit who brings Ezekiel to the valley. The Hebrew word *ruach* is woven throughout the Dry Bones story with its three-fold meaning of breath, spirit, and wind. All relate to the presence and life-power of God. The Lord speaks and acts. The Lord is a commanding presence, fully engaged and in control of the situation. This would be reassurance to a defeated, dispersed, and captive people. Three times in the story Ezekiel is addressed by God as "mortal,"[3] emphasizing the radical distance between the two characters of the story.

Bones are a principal object in the story. They are introduced with the emphasis of a short, slow sentence as the climax of an episode: "It was full of bones." In the second episode their number is emphasized ("there were very many of them") as is their condition ("they were very dry"). The latter comes at the end of the episode in another short, climatic phrase that warrants a significant pause in the telling to allow the image to sink in. These dry bones are the object of the Lord's attention, message, and action. Their number, their dryness, their being strewn about unburied, their description as "these slain," all point to a history of violence.

In the last part of the story the Lord identifies the bones as the "whole house of Israel"—that is, all the people who have been divided and dispersed through years of war. Further, the Lord identifies their communal state of mind as lacking power ("our bones are dried up"), hope ("our hope is gone"), and connection ("we are cut off completely"). God telling what the bones say cleverly communicates the inside view of an entire nation of people. Who can argue with divine perception? In the concluding episode of the story, the Lord references another object closely related to dry bones: graves.

The plot of the story unfolds quite logically:

Part 1. Ezekiel has a spirit-inspired experience of being set down in the middle of a wide valley filled with dry bones, and moving among them. The dilemma of the story is established when the Lord asks him if the bones can live. Ezekiel wisely defers to the Lord's judgment about that.

Part 2. Ezekiel is told to prophecy to the bones that they will be restored to new life with breath, sinews, flesh, and skin. He does, and the bones come together with sinews, flesh and skin, but without breath.

Part 3. Ezekiel is told to prophecy to the breath. He does, and the breath enters. The "vast multitude" then stand on their feet. These are not zombies; they are fully alive with the spirit of God breathed into them.

Part 4. The Lord interprets who these bones are and how they feel, announcing what will be done about it and what will be the result. The Lord will put the Lord's spirit in them, restore them to their land, and expect them to realize the divine source of their redemption. The

3. Other translations use "son of man" or "mortal man" which have the disadvantage of patriarchal language but are more consistent with the original language.

question raised in Part 1 about whether or not the bones could live is answered in the affirmative.

Norms of judgment present in this story revolve around the bones as remains of dead bodies that were not properly buried. Ancient sensibilities about clean and unclean would come into play here. Along with being a symbol of death, the scattered bones represent a state of gross uncleanness. The concept of being unclean was connected in the previous story with the people's unfaithfulness to God. Their promised cleansing was attributed exclusively to the will and work of God: "I will sprinkle clean water upon you, and you shall be clean from all your uncleannesses" (Ezek 36:25).

In the same way, the defilement of death will be removed by the freely given Spirit of God. It is the obedience of the prophet in telling the message he is commanded to tell that makes possible the opportunity for new life, the restoration of hope, and the return to community. The vocation of biblical storytelling with incarcerated men and women continues such prophetic obedience.

The Storyteller

The following section will identify in detail the possible gestures, tempo, and attitudes used by a storyteller telling the story of Dry Bones.

Part 1. Especially if the telling venue is a small room, the storyteller[4] might begin from a seated position. She speaks in a calm, steady, strong voice to deliver the line known to signify an impending experience with God: "The hand of the LORD came upon me." There is no eye contact with the audience as the storyteller enters a kind of trance such as Ezekiel would have experienced. This line might be accompanied by a raised arm out-stretched with palm down, slowly moving up and down, then moving back to open up a vision of the valley. While the arm lowers to the side, a long dramatic pause allows the storyteller and the audience to look in that space between them established as the valley. Then the storyteller might connect with the audience through eye contact while delivering the climactic sentence slowly with emphasis and a sense of horror: "It was full of bones."

As the second episode begins, the storyteller returns to her introspective state, looking down at the bones. She moves her arm in a figure eight

---

4. The storyteller will be referenced as female for this story and as male for the following story, Behind Locked Doors.

to indicate being led all around them. The episode ends with a sigh of deep sorrow accompanying the short, concluding sentence: "And they were very dry." The phrase is said slowly, dirge-like. The eyes are downcast, the posture drooping.

Both the tempo and the tone pick up when the Lord starts speaking in episode 3. The storyteller might experiment with different volumes to see what fits best. It could be a soft voice, almost a whisper. Or it could be a come-to-attention voice, drawing the storyteller and audience out of their sorrow. The spine straightens and the head comes up, perhaps with a sideways tilt and glance to indicate the question from one to another. Ezekiel's response is delivered with a shake of the head, perhaps another sigh and a tone of doubtful resignation. There is no eye contact with the audience during this episode which depicts dialogue between the Lord and the prophet.

Part 2. The phrase "Then the Lord GOD said to me" begins each of the remaining three parts of the story. It is said quickly in a neutral voice as Ezekiel recounts what happened. The instructions to prophesy which follow are vocalized with clear articulation, moderate speed, and an everything-is-under-control-here attitude. The hand might be raised in a stylized rhetorical gesture, bringing it down during the brief pause before the next episode.

The second episode of part 2 begins at a slow pace with emphasis on the word "breath." The hand might stretch out from the mouth toward the audience at an angle. Emphasis continues on each word of the conclusion of that sentence, especially the last one: "and . . . you . . . shall . . . LIVE." This clause is a verbal thread repeated at the end of the next sentence, twice in episode three with slight variations, and again word-for-word at the end of the story. The message is not to be missed and the promise is sure. The attitude to convey here and again throughout the story is, "I am the Lord and there is no question about this happening if I say it will happen."

The sentence about the sinews, flesh, skin, and breath is a long one and so moves along quickly, perhaps accompanied by gestures of stroking alternate arms. The sequence of body parts can be remembered by thinking from the inside out: bones, sinews (tendons), flesh (muscles), all covered by skin and animated by breath. "And you shall know that I am the Lord" is a verbal thread connecting this beginning of God's Word in the story to its ending. It should be said with the same no-nonsense attitude mentioned above.

The ball is now back in Ezekiel's court. It is easy to remember the next episode because it follows so logically on the heels of God's command: "So I prophesied as I had been commanded." This line presents an opportunity for the storyteller to reconnect with the audience. A bit of lightness could be introduced into this otherwise heavy story by the enthusiasm and energy of compliance. The storyteller wants to be sure the audience knows that she, as Ezekiel, has done what she was told.

In the remainder of the episode the storyteller, portraying Ezekiel's perspective, describes what happened as a result of the prophesying with increasing volume, speed and amazement. First she describes something heard (cock the head in a gesture of listening, bring the fingers together to indicate the coming together of the bones), then something seen (repeat the gestures accompanying the repeated words about sinews, flesh, and skin). The vocalization radically downshifts with the concluding phrase of part 2: "But there was no breath in them." This is said quietly, slowly, with an air of disappointment. The storyteller looks at the audience sadly shaking her head.

Part 3. This is the shortest part of the story, easy for the storyteller to remember because it follows the same pattern as the previous part: instruction to prophesy, compliance, and results. The use of voice and gesture may also follow suit with "the breath came into them" delivered in even greater amazement than the coming of sinews, etc. The next phrase—"and stood on their feet"—is an obvious invitation for the storyteller to stand up and also to indicate by gesture (raise both arms) for the audience to stand up.

For the remainder of the story the storyteller maintains eye contact with the audience. They become the "vast multitude" (spoken slowly with great emphasis) when the storyteller widens her outstretched arms and moves her body in a scan to include them all. The stage is now set for the final powerful scene of the story.

Part 4. The words of God addressed to Ezekiel at the beginning of part 4 are delivered in a manner that maintains the audience's identity as the people of Israel in exile. "Mortal, these bones are the whole house of Israel . . ." is spoken like an explanatory aside, though one directed not by the storyteller to the audience, but rather one delivered by God to Ezekiel. This is accomplished by gesturing toward the audience in a listening stance and speaking God's words in a gentle tone. "And they say . . ." introduces the ultimate inside view: God speaking what is on the hearts of the people.

When the Lord quotes the people, the storyteller might invite audience members to repeat "Our bones are dried up . . ." This will deepen audience identification with the people of Israel, already established in the act of standing, and set them up for a powerful experience of God's redemptive love in the concluding episodes. The three laments should be said with increasing distress. Be prepared for the repeating to continue beyond the laments unless there is an obvious cue to stop audience response. If the repeating does continue, as was the case in the jail telling, there will be a mutual benediction. The storyteller speaking as God to the audience blesses them with the promise of new life. The audience speaking as God to the storyteller blesses her with the same promise.

The command to prophesy with its familiar phrases is delivered as before. But the tone changes with the actual prophecy that runs through the rest of the story. The distance is closed between God and God's people through the incredible, beautiful promises God makes. The storyteller's tone conveys both the power and the compassion of God's unconditional love, especially poignant in the repeated phrase "O my people." It is said very slowly, like a caress, the second time. Appropriate gestures are graceful, full-arm movements indicating opening graves, bringing up from graves, and bringing back to the land. The hand to the heart with a soft pat could compliment the phrase "I will put my spirit within you." In delivering the last line with full audience engagement, the storyteller should muster up her strongest faith conviction about divine will, power, steadfast mercy, and everlasting love.

The Audience

The original context for this story was summarized in the introduction to this chapter: the days of the Babylonian exile in the sixth century BCE when it seemed to the Israelites that all had been lost through the violence of war and the greed of empire. The original audiences of this story were people who had experienced the loss of family, friends, leaders, homes, and freedom. Their holy city and its glorious temple lay in ruins along with their way of life. God seemed either absent or powerless. Belief systems that had worked to make sense of reality had apparently failed.

This story begins in a place of death, a condition of permanent uncleanness, a valley of dry bones. The original audience had been conquered and exiled by a Gentile enemy. The connections would be immediately apparent to them. They may be offended or pained at the reminder of their situation, but more likely will appreciate its exposure, especially when visited by the Lord and the prophet's attention. Previously in the epic the audience has received explanation for their situation: a consequence of breaking God's laws.

The unfolding drama of this story gives the audience a reason to hope for the possibility of new life. That hope is grounded in the power, will, and love of God for them, as communicated through the prophet/storyteller. The audience is encouraged to experience God's presence along with Ezekiel, to hear God's voice delivered by the storyteller, to trust God's power and promises, and, finally, to feel God's love. All that God does is credited to God's desire that the people know God. God *is*, and God *is for* them.

This story is all about dynamics of distance between the immortality of God and the mortality of the audience. The starting point is extreme distance. The Lord is away; the audience is invited to observe a field of bones. Because of the norm of judgment about uncleanness associated with dead bodies, the original audience would have felt alienated by the vision, perhaps aghast that the Lord and Ezekiel were moving all around those bones. To the extent that the audience identifies with the bones they are also distanced from the Holy One. During the course of the story the distance of relationship with God decreases because: (1) the bones take on life, (2) the audience is directly addressed as the bones/people, (3) God demonstrates inside knowledge of the people's emotions, and (4) God's address becomes increasingly intimate.

At the end of the story, God is still completely *other*, but the distance has been eliminated at God's initiative by God's indwelling spirit. The impact of the story is most likely the experience of forgiveness for breaking God's laws and of restoration to right relationship. It is the relief of despair by a new source of hope, a breath of divine air for dry bones. The story invites the audience to consider both the nature and the sources of their hopes. It encourages the audience to recall the disasters of their life, which left them lying like so many dry bones slain in a valley, and to reflect on their degree of trust in God to bring new life out of those disasters. The strongest invitation is to experience the presence and power of God within their own being, bringing hope with each breath. They can be invited to notice their own breath.

Many of these same dynamics are readily experienced by audiences today, especially audiences of incarcerated persons. They, too, have been captured and taken away from their community. They have lost friends and family by being locked away; some have lost them through rejection. Their situation is a result of society's judgment that they have disobeyed the law.

Many experience depression ("our bones are dried up"), hopelessness ("our hope is gone"), and lonely isolation ("we are cut off completely"). The story can have a similar impact on this audience as it had on the original one.

The possibility of these connections was actualized when this story was told to a circle of nine women in jail. Following the telling, a "check-in" round elicited these responses: "The story evoked emotion—God can do that for me"; "I feel blessed—my dry bones are living for Christ"; "I am feeling grateful; I was depressed, now I'm back to an upswing." One woman reflected with a tone of scandal about her self-destructive behavior and then expressed hope that God might give her new life, too. Interestingly, while the inmates responded in these ways, the outside co-leader most strongly connected with the final line (as did the storyteller) expressing frustration with all the injustices in today's world and wishing that God would, indeed, *act* to do something about them.

A tragic connection of this story with contemporary experience is "the killing fields" of Cambodia. From 1974–1979 an estimated one and a half to two million people were executed by the Khmer Rouge and buried in mass graves. One of these sites is now a memorial to the suffering experienced by the people of Cambodia: Choeung Ek near the capital city of Phnom Penh. The centerpiece is a large Buddhist stupa filled with layers of skulls of the victims. A person walking around the shallow graves of the killing fields may encounter clothes and bones that continue to surface during heavy rains. It is an all too literal experience of the valley of dry bones which Ezekiel described. Nevertheless, Cambodia, like Israel, has experienced new life. While still challenged with many struggles, Cambodia is a vibrant and hopeful country.

There are those in jail or prison who can identify with Ezekiel. They can provide a prophetic witness to God's Word. Ezekiel was one of the exiles, a captive experiencing all the pain that other exiles suffered. He was a leader chosen by God who accepted the calling to prophesy judgment for wrongs done in the past. In this story he follows the divine directive to prophesy confidence in a just, attentive, and active God whose Spirit breathes new life into defeated people. Through learning, telling, and teaching the stories of God, inmates can be like Ezekiel, both for the sake of those inside and, upon release, for the sake of those back in their home communities.

BEHIND LOCKED DOORS (JOHN 20:19–23)

The Story

When it was evening on that day, the first day of the week,
>and the doors of the house where the disciples had met were locked
>>for fear of the Judeans,
>Jesus came and stood among them and says, "Peace be with you."
Having said this, he showed them his hands and his side.

Then the disciples rejoiced when they saw the Lord.
Jesus said to them again, "Peace be with you.
As the Father has sent me, so I send you."

When he had said this, he breathed on them and says to them,
>"Receive the Holy Spirit.
If you forgive the sins of any, they are forgiven them.
If you retain the sins of any, they are retained."

～

This transcription of the story varies from its NRSV translation in two significant ways. Both variations change the meaning of the story. In the opening sentence the Greek word *Ioudaioi* is translated "Judeans" rather than "Jews." This word change is made for the sake of greater historical accuracy. It is also made to avoid anti-Semitic interpretations for which John's Gospel is infamous, and which were not originally intended. As articulated by Bruce Malina and Richard Rohrbaugh in their study of John from the perspective of social sciences, the twenty-first-century understanding of the meaning of the word "Jews" is significantly different than that of the first century. Of the seventy instances in John where the term appears, they write:

> there is nothing of the modern connotations of "Jew" or "Jewishness." Hence, it is simply inappropriate to project those modern meanings backward into the period when John was written. Rather, Judean meant a person belonging to a group called Judeans, situated geographically and forming a territory taking its name

from its inhabitants, Judea . . . The correlatives of Judean in John
are "Galilean" and "Perean," and together they make up Israel.[5]

David Ewart, a United Church of Christ minister in Vancouver, British Columbia, succinctly summarizes the case for the word change on his website: www.holytextures.com. He presses further for the use of "Judean authorities" to bring even more clarity.[6]

The second change in translation is a literal translation of the historical present tense, restoring its use in the original Greek. This grammatical construction is present in two of the introductions to Jesus' speech but has been eliminated in the NRSV because of high literate sensibilities. The historical present tense creates a sense of immediacy and is commonly used in everyday storytelling. Both usages in Behind Locked Doors occur in introductions to Jesus' speech: "says" rather than "said" (John 20:19, 22). Use of the historical present tense brings the past into the present where the story is most likely to be experienced as relevant to the lives of its audience.[7]

A third way in which sound maps frequently differ from the NRSV is with regard to punctuation. The original Greek transcription of the stories was not punctuated, nor were upper case letters used to designate the beginning of a new sentence. Scripts developed for oral storytelling differ in formatting from the literate structure of modern Bibles like the NRSV. Commonly, literary translations break up the long sentences (periods) characteristic of orality.

In Greek the conjunction *kai* (usually translated "and") is often used to keep the momentum building with a series of connected phrases (cola) that are all part of one long sentence (period). High-literates avoid such constructions in written documents, considering them "run-on" sentences in English. Translators frequently break the phrases into separate sentences. In storytelling, however, a string of phrases functions as a series of breath units. In this case, the building excitement of an extended series of cola in the original Greek is maintained.

---

5. Malina and Rohrbaugh, *Social-Science Commentary on John*, 44–45. The territory is specifically "located in the southern and western part of the Roman province of Syria-Palestine."

6. Ewart, "It's 'Judeans' not 'Jews.'"

7. I am indebted to Phil Ruge-Jones for teaching me about the historical present tense and its use in this story. See his performance criticism commentary on John 20:19–31, "Mentored into Steadfast Love," 4.

This story is one of several about Jesus' post-resurrection appearances. It follows the report of what happened at the tomb on the morning of Jesus' resurrection. It is immediately preceded by Mary's announcement to the disciples, "I have seen the Lord!" It describes what happened on the evening of that same day. It is followed by the story of how Thomas came to see the risen Jesus a week later and was convinced that his resurrection really occurred.

This is a one-scene, three-episode story with two characters. One character is Jesus; the other is a composite character, the disciples. The story is structured around three plot movements initiated by Jesus. Episode 1 establishes the setting, introduces the characters and gives the first plot movement. Episode 2 describes the disciples' response to Jesus' unexpected appearance, and relates Jesus' next action. Episode 3 concludes the story with a final act of Jesus.

The story is set in the evening on "that day"—a reference to the previous story about Mary encountering the risen Christ at the tomb. A follow-up phrase about it being "the first day of the week" emphasizes the day. In modern terms, it is Sunday evening. The scene takes place in the room where the disciples were gathered.

Jesus is the main character in this story as he is the main character in the Gospel of John. He has been described over the course of the epic with a number of powerful metaphors such as the Word, the light of the world, the lamb of God, the good shepherd, and the true vine. Jesus is a teacher, a healer, and a purveyor of signs. Many of his followers think he is the one God has chosen to deliver them from Roman domination—the Messiah—though they misunderstand what kind of messiah he will be. They want a messiah like David who will destroy enemies. Jesus is a messiah who overcomes enemies with love. He offends and frightens the Judean authorities with his words, actions, and loyal following.

Because Jesus is a threat to the prevailing political order, he is opposed and arrested by the Judean religious leaders and handed over to be executed by the Romans as a would-be "king of the Judeans." In other words, he was treated as an insurrectionist. In the course of the execution his hands were mutilated by being nailed to a cross and his side was pierced with a spear. In the world of this story it is now the third day after his death. The resurrected Jesus has already conversed with Mary Magdalene and has sent her to tell his disciples about his impending ascension.

Despite this good news, the disciples are sequestered behind locked doors. It is assumed that this group of disciples is Jesus' inner circle—those he called, taught, and lived with in his traveling school—minus Thomas (the next story describes his absence) and Judas (who having betrayed Jesus is now gone). Unlike the epics told by Matthew and Mark, John does not describe the disciples running away after Jesus' arrest. We do know, however, that they have gathered in this room and locked the doors because they are afraid. It is a safe assumption that the disciples are afraid they will be arrested and perhaps executed, as was their teacher. Even though at their last supper together Jesus gave a long discourse meant to prepare them spiritually and psychologically for this situation, and even though Mary has informed them that Jesus has been raised from the dead, the disciples are hiding fearfully behind locked doors.

The doors function as an important detail in the story because their being locked provides an inside view of the disciples' emotional state. They are afraid of the men who instigated their teacher's death. Locked doors also function to highlight the supernatural aspect of Jesus. His presence with them is not inhibited by physical factors. He can suddenly appear in their midst despite locked doors. The image is somewhat like the teleportation phenomenon of "Star Trek" fame.[8]

A norm of judgment operating in this story is that students obey their teachers and trust their teachings. Earlier in the Gospel Jesus had spoken to his disciples at length about what was about to happen and how God would help them cope (John 13:31—17:26). He had spoken clearly about how he would soon leave them. He promised to send them an advocate, the Holy Spirit. He had made every effort to prepare them for the challenges of the future, to console them beforehand for their impending loss, to assure them they would not be left alone without guidance, and to encourage them to remain faithful despite adversity.

In the last supper discourse, Jesus offered peace to his disciples and then addressed the issue of fear head-on: "Do not let your hearts be troubled, and do not let them be afraid" (John 14:27). Consequently, the original audience might have judged the disciples negatively for being afraid.

---

8. As an aside, "Beam me up, Scotty" was never actually said in any Star Trek television series or film. Like other famous misquotations that can be verified through audiovisual evidence, it is a product of secondary oral culture. This contemporary phenomenon provides an interesting example of the dynamics of the primary oral culture which gave us our biblical tradition. For details on the Star Trek phrase, see http://www.todayifoundout.com/index.php/2013/10/beam-scotty-never-said-original-star-trek.

They might have thought poorly of the disciples' hiding out behavior in light of their teacher's eloquent discourse in his last hours with them, just three days earlier. But the audience could also empathize with the disciples' fear. They were all too familiar with Roman brutality.

The three movements of the plot, corresponding with the three episodes of the story, are as follows:

Episode 1: Jesus Appears. Jesus appears in the room with his frightened disciples, greets them, and shows them his hands and his side. Why does he do this? Presumably it proves to them it is really him, Jesus, their beloved teacher who was recently crucified.

Episode 2: Jesus Commissions. The natural consequence of the first plot movement is that the disciples rejoice. Jesus then repeats what he just said and adds a commission: "As the Father has sent me, so I send you."

Episode 3: Jesus Empowers. The third plot movement is Jesus breathing on his disciples with the interpretive statement—"Receive the Holy Spirit"—which empowers them to fulfill the commission he has just administered. The story concludes with a descriptive statement about their power to forgive.

A significant verbal thread in this story is the phrase, "Peace be with you," which ties together the first two episodes. Its use in episode 1 could simply be a standard ancient near eastern salutation. It does, however, carry overtones of the gift of peace Jesus offered his disciples at the last supper (John 14:27). It also points back to the concluding exhortation of that discourse: "I have said this to you, so that in me you may have peace" (John 16:33).

In episode 2, the exact repetition of the phrase, "Peace be with you," indicates that Jesus is saying something much weightier than a simple greeting. He is, in fact, reminding them of all he said to them before, emphasizing the truth of what he said before, and again both offering and exhorting peace. The disciples need not be anxious, afraid, or vengeful.

Jesus' commissioning of the disciples is a verbal thread to the "high priestly prayer" in which he says, "As you have sent me into the world, so I have sent them into the world" (John 17:18). In that instance he is talking to God about the disciples and describing an action he has already taken. Now, in his post-resurrection appearance he speaks directly to the disciples:

"As the Father has sent me, so I send you." Surely they will pay attention and believe him this time.

The Hebrew word *ruach* and the Greek word *pneuma*, have the same range of meanings: breath, wind, and spirit. Ezekiel plays on this multivalency in the story of Dry Bones. John takes advantage of it as well, both in the story of Nicodemus at the beginning of his gospel, and in this story near its end. The verbal thread between breath and spirit in episode 3 is lost in English, but the connections are not lost to the promise of the Holy Spirit in Jesus' last supper discourse. For those in John's audiences who were steeped in the scriptures this image of a divine figure breathing on despairing people to instill them with the spirit for the sake of new life would also have been a verbal thread connecting John's Gospel with Ezekiel's prophecy.

The mention of Jesus' hands and side connects this story with that of his death, thereby reminding the audience of the role of the Judean authorities. The disciples' fear was understandable. The mention of hands and side also provides a reminder that Jesus definitely died. The Judean authorities asked Pilate to have the legs of the three crucified men broken so that they would die and their bodies could be removed before the Sabbath. The soldiers followed Pilate's orders and broke the legs of the men crucified on either side of Jesus, but when they came to Jesus they found he was already dead. So instead of breaking his legs, they pierced his side with a spear (John 19:31–37).

The Storyteller

Episode 1. The storyteller begins telling the story in a neutral tone at a medium pace. The pitch will probably drop in the explanation of the time with a knowing tone, emphasizing that the impending action will take place at the same time early Christian communities gathered to worship: the evening of the first day of the week. The pitch then resumes its initial level. The phrase about the doors being locked is conveyed with mild intensity reflecting the danger the disciples are in. In contrast, as the narrator brings Jesus into the story, his tone is one of increasing amazement and joy, accompanied by an increase in volume and tempo.

The storyteller's gestures and movement might include:

- *first day of the week*—a shift of the body toward the audience, raising the hand close to the chest and slightly punctuating the words;

- *were locked*—striking one open hand with the fist of the other;
- *stood among them*—moving arms down and slightly out in front toward audience (to help them identify with the disciples), palms facing audience and fingers together;
- *"Peace be with you"*—raising one hand in a stylized gesture of greeting/blessing, direct eye contact with the audience;
- *his hands and his side*—showing hands to the audience, then placing hand lightly on the side.

Episode 2. After a pause allowing the scene to unfold in the imagination of the audience, the storyteller resumes the story in a celebrative tone with high energy to describe the disciples' joyful response to seeing the Lord. He might interrupt the narration with clapping and cheering and invite the audience to join in the celebration.

When the time seems right, the storyteller resumes in a calm, quiet, but loving tone, accompanied with a smile, to deliver Jesus' repetition of "Peace be with you." The storyteller engages the audience with direct eye contact as before, taking time to scan the audience. The words are the same, but are spoken more slowly and with greater emphasis, to capture the full attention of the audience for the commissioning which follows. This time "Peace be with you" may be accompanied by a gesture of both hands up with palms facing the audience. "As the Father has sent me, so I send you" can be accompanied by gestures first toward the self, then toward the audience.

Episode 3. The storyteller narrates the action of the last part of the story in the neutral style with which he began. Before saying "he breathed on them" the storyteller may want to pause, take a deep breath, and quietly exhale—just a suggestion of the action, not an attempt to re-create it. Eye contact with the audience is established and maintained through the end of the story.

The last two lines about forgiving or retaining sins are delivered with calm and sobriety, but with nuanced differences. The line about forgiveness of sins might be said with warmth, accompanied by a slight smile and a gesture of open hands. The line about retention of sins would be said with less warmth, no smile and a tone communicating "this will be a problem." In an accompanying gesture, the storyteller might close his hands into fists and then cross his arms across his body.

The Audience

In traditional exegetical work the audience of John has been assumed to be Gentile Christian readers. A new understanding of the audience has developed through biblical performance criticism and experiential exegesis. Analysis of the Gospel of John from this perspective yields a different picture of the constituency of the original audience and of how they experienced John's story about Jesus.

Study of the interwoven dynamics of audience address and identity led Boomershine to conclude, "Insofar as our goal is to understand and interpret the Fourth Gospel in its original historical context, it is essential to hear the story as performed for audiences that were predominantly composed of late-first-century Jews."[9] The original meaning of John's Gospel is at many points quite different when the story is understood as a live performance experienced by an attentive group of Judeans, rather than a book read by individual Gentiles.

What, then, were some general characteristics of this late-first-century Judean audience? By the time John's story of Jesus was in circulation in the last decade of the first century, the sons and daughters of Abraham and Sarah had once again experienced the total destruction of their holy city, their temple, and their way of life. It happened during the previous generation, some twenty to thirty years earlier. They lived in an unstable and uncertain environment. As in the days of Ezekiel, many had been killed. During the Judean-Roman war, estimates are one to one and a half million Judeans were killed. Many others were enslaved. At best, they were at risk of cultural assimilation; at worst, they suffered persecution and death.

Jesus' action showing his hands and side is a vivid reminder to the audience of his crucifixion, of Roman domination, and of the complicity of Judean religious authorities in Jesus' time. Like their forebears during the Babylonian exile and Jesus' first disciples, this was an audience who had experienced death. Many were locked up in fear and despair. Others were imprisoned by anger and the desire for revenge. Still others were held captive by the turmoil of anxiety.

In the story of Behind Locked Doors the risen Jesus is once again addressing his beloved disciples. First-century audiences, experiencing the story as oral storytelling, might initially be distanced from the disciples because of their fear and lack of trust. But when Jesus suddenly appears

9. Boomershine, "The Medium and Message of John," 120.

and greets them lovingly that distance collapses. They are invited into close identification with the disciples and experience the storyteller as Jesus speaking to them as his disciples. Boomershine describes this phenomenon and explains how it impacts the audience:

> The impact of the story is to engage the audience in a dynamic and passionate interaction with Jesus as a character who directly addressed them throughout the story. The message implicit in the Gospel was to appeal to Judean listeners to move through the conflicts of engagement with Jesus to belief in Jesus as the Messiah.[10]

Somehow this "belief in Jesus as the Messiah" had to overcome the daunting evidence to the contrary implicit in his crucifixion and death.

First-century audiences in the ancient near east were all too familiar with crucifixion. According to Jodi Magness, crucifixion was a punishment inflicted by Romans on "rebellious provincials for incitement to rebellion and acts of treason, whom they considered common 'bandits.'"[11] Its intent was control by terror, much as lynching served to control African Americans in recent history. Magness describes how it was accomplished: "by spreading apart the arms of a live victim, so that he/she could be affixed to the crossbeam by ropes or nails."[12] The person was left there until he could no longer hold himself up to breathe. Jesus had been nailed to a crossbeam, the evidence of which he showed on his hands. He indicated the reality of his death by showing his side.

This evidence—wounds to hands and side—does not lead audience members to dwell on the horror of crucifixion. Insofar as they identify with the disciples they see it as evidence of his resurrection. They also rejoice, as the experience of Jesus as the risen Messiah sinks in. The strength of the impact of this particular story depends in part upon how much of the complete Gospel the audience has experienced. Have they heard his call, witnessed his signs, and listened to his teaching?

Original audiences would have experienced all this in an oral performance of the entire epic. The audience remembers how Jesus had told them, "You heard me say to you, 'I am going away, and I am coming to you.' If you loved me you would rejoice that I am going to the Father, because the Father is greater than I" (John 14:28). Now the audience might follow Jesus' suggestion: they rejoice as Jesus' disciples.

10. Ibid., 94.
11. Magness, *Stone and Dung, Oil and Spit*, 166.
12. Ibid., 167.

This prepares the audience to hear—and this time to truly believe—Jesus' subsequent words of peace, commissioning, and empowerment. In the wake of all that happened in the world outside their small community of faith, the followers of Jesus could not comply with his instructions when he was with them the first time. He has come again, in resurrected form, to instruct again: "Don't be anxious, be at peace. Calm your fears and your anger, be at peace. Go into the world as I have to demonstrate God's powerful love."

Not only does Jesus repeat his message, he also performs an act: he breathes on them. The original audience, whose sacred scriptural tradition at this point is the law and the prophets, would likely be well acquainted with how in the beginning God breathed life into the human God created (Gen 2:7), and how in the exile God's spirit breathed life into dry bones. In the sixth century BCE, during the exile, there emerged a new understanding of God, a new way of living faithfully within a hostile environment, and a new means of worship apart from the Temple. In the centuries after the exile, from dry bones strewn in a valley of violence came the synagogue and Sabbath piety.

In the aftermath of the Roman-Judean war, once again there emerged a fresh understanding of God, a new means of worship without the temple, and a new way of living faithfully. From a handful of frightened people came the Gospels and the church. John's story of Jesus appearing to his disciples on the evening of his resurrection empowered those developments. It enabled the audience to perceive Jesus as the Messiah who brings peace inside locked doors for the sake of peace everywhere. It brought them joy, revived their hopes, strengthened their spirits, and compelled them to act.

Those who heard this story were commissioned to go out into the world as Jesus' disciples had, with words of reconciliation and acts of mercy. In order to do this they needed the power of forgiveness, both for wrong-doings they had committed and for wrong-doings they had suffered. Jesus' final words in this story have been interpreted as a mandate for the Roman Catholic Church's authority to forgive sins. This became a divisive issue during the Reformation.[13] An alternative understanding, gleaned from listening to the story as story, is that Jesus is presenting an important choice

13. A description of this interpretation and the arguments about it between Protestants and Catholics is outlined in Raymond Brown's commentary on the Gospel of John. See Brown, *John*, 1041.

that the disciples (and hence the audience) will make.[14] In succinct language he describes the dynamics of the possible responses to wrong-doing: letting go or holding on. Those who forgive wrong-doing will be freed from the bondage of fear, shame, and anger. Those who hold on to the effects of wrong-doing will remain in bondage to them and inflict them on others.

The Horizon Prison Initiative in Ohio describes this dynamic succinctly: "Trauma not treated is trauma transferred." The first disciples and other first-century Judeans all experienced trauma at the hand of the Romans. Jesus breathed on them and told them to receive the Holy Spirit, who gives them the ability to forgive, should they so choose.

Connections to this story for those who are incarcerated are similar to connections with the Dry Bones story, if not even more obvious. Telling the story in a small locked room to a small group of jailed women creates a powerful setting for Jesus' appearance and greeting of peace. Whether or not they are familiar with the Gospel (and many are not) the direct connections of locked doors, fear, and the need for peace puts them in a position to be strongly impacted by this story. When asked what gesture to use with the last line about retaining sins the women immediately put their hands behind their backs as if they were handcuffed. When asked to tell their stories of locking doors out of fear, they readily told stories about barricading bedroom doors to keep out men, or because a relative had been shot or a neighbor attacked.

In many ways incarcerated persons have experiences that are like those of the original audience:

- Old way of life disrupted or altogether gone
- Loss of family and friends
- An uncertain future
- Temptations and threats within and without
- Embedded memory of trauma
- Experiences of guilt, shame, and humiliation
- Domination by the criminal justice system

Most women and men in jail or prison have experienced abuse themselves and often have transferred that abuse to others. Jesus' words about forgiveness connect with their experience.

---

14. Boomershine, "A Storytelling Commentary on John 20:19–31."

Some of those participating in Circle of the Word have been part of a faith community and now seek renewed commitment. All of the participants in a Circle of the Word need a source of meaning and empowerment. That need can be met if they experience Jesus breathing his spirit onto them and sending them out to share God's love with cellmates, guards, and families. The story of the resurrected Jesus appearing to his frightened disciples in the aftermath of his execution is a potential resource to address many of the spiritual needs and desires of people living, literally, behind locked doors.

5

Pioneers of Prison Ministry

"THE ATTENTION OF ANGELS"

In June of 1822 the American politician John Randolph[1] traveled to England and introduced himself to a Quaker minister named Elizabeth Fry. Mrs. Fry was getting ready to visit women at Newgate Prison. She "was so extremely pleased with his most original conversation"[2] that she took him along. Two days later Mr. Randolph told an acquaintance about his experience:

> I saw the greatest curiosity in London; aye, and in England, too, sir—compared to which, Westminster Abbey, the Tower, Somerset House, the British Museum, nay Parliament itself, sink into utter insignificance! I have seen, sir, Elizabeth Fry, of Newgate, and I have witnessed there, sir, miraculous effects of true Christianity upon the most depraved of human beings ... Oh! Sir, it was a sight worthy the attention of angels![3]

Perhaps it was this effusive description of Mrs. Fry which inspired Edward Ryder to quote the King James Version of Matthew 26:13 on the title page

---

1. John Randolph was a Congressional representative from Virginia at the time, later Senator and minister to Russia; cousin of Thomas Jefferson and radical proponent of states' rights.

2. Garland, *Life of John Randolph*, 186.

3. Ibid., 185.

of his 1883 biography: "Verily I say unto you, Wheresoever this gospel shall be preached in the whole world, there shall also this, that this woman hath done, be told for a memorial of her."[4] It is hard to imagine higher praise than comparison to the woman who anointed Jesus (Mark 14:9).

Thanks to a lifelong discipline of keeping a journal and two daughters who published them posthumously, we have access to the interior life of Elizabeth Fry. And so we can know with relative certainty that she would have had mixed feelings about such extravagant praise. On the one hand, she needed signs of acceptance and affirmation from her fellow humans, both for her own peace of mind and for the sake of the causes to which she devoted her life. On the other hand, Elizabeth was ever on guard against temptations to pride and believed that God, not she, was due all credit for good results.

Certainly she would have objected to Randolph's characterization of the women she visited as "depraved" and "worse, if possible, than the devil himself." Her references to female inmates were always accompanied with compassion and understanding. These objections aside, Randolph rightly named the event he witnessed. What happened at Newgate and in prisons throughout the Western world due to the work of Elizabeth Fry is indeed "worthy the attention of angels"—and also of humans.

Those who went before her laid the foundation. During the eighteenth century, Christian conviction mobilized certain persons to engage in dangerous, distasteful, and difficult challenges regarding the criminal justice system and those subject to its machinery. They represented a broad spectrum of the British Protestant community: Anglican, Methodist, Congregationalist, and Quaker. Knowing the stories of Elizabeth Fry's predecessors contributes to understanding and appreciating her work.

This chapter will examine the ways in which the Christian community in Enlightenment England tackled the issues of prison and prisoners, with a particular focus on the work of Elizabeth Fry. The work over time has transformed institutions in England and elsewhere, with new norms established for human behavior regarding imprisonment. Their influence is felt to this day, as is the need for their on-going witness, as attitudes and practices they challenged continually reassert themselves.[5]

---

4. Ibid., 185–86.

5. Three examples are: the death penalty, extended solitary confinement, and the practice of torture to extract confessions or information.

MR. SHUTE AND THE SPCK: "A BIBLE TO EVERY CHAMBER"

The seventeenth century was a time of great change in European culture. In the wake of the Protestant Reformation and the religious wars that ensued, England was searching for new grounding of belief and morality upon which all could agree. Protestants looked to the Bible for authority, but the Bible was open to so many interpretations that they splintered into more and more factions.

All assumptions about the nature of things went up for grabs, including basic belief in revelation.[6] Christian piety waned, along with regard for religious learning and traditional guidelines for ethical behavior. Vice was perceived as increasing to alarming levels. A causal relationship was made between the prevalence of immoral behavior and the lack of religious education. Regardless of whether morality and Christian education were significantly less during the seventeenth century than during other centuries, concern for these factors motivated the formation of an organization meant to address them.

In 1698 the Society for Promoting Christian Knowledge (SPCK) was founded by five members of the Church of England: one clergyman, two lawyers, one nobleman, and "a country gentleman of some distinction."[7] Its agenda included the establishment of "charity schools" for children of parents who could not afford to pay for education. There was no such thing as government-funded "public education" in seventeenth-century England. As a result, a high percentage of the populace, and especially of the poor, were illiterate. The rationale for the establishment of charity schools was, according to a nineteenth-century analysis, the need for Christian education. According to this analysis, "the growth of vice and debauchery is greatly owing to the gross ignorance of the principles of the Christian Religion, especially among the poorer sort."[8]

For similar reasons, English prisons were a second target of the SPCK in its formative stage. At the meeting of the Society on February 22, 1699, a lecturer at Whitechapel identified simply as "Mr. Shute" reported on conditions in London prisons and proposed reforms. Whitechapel was in East London, by this time a place of poverty and destitution, which may explain

6. Allen and McClure, *Two Hundred Years*, 1.

7. Ibid., 13.

8. Ibid., 27.

Mr. Shute's involvement. It is reputed that Compton, the Anglican Bishop of London, recommended an investigation into prison conditions that led to Mr. Shute's report.[9] The report was the fruit of discourse with the "Ordinary" (chaplain) of Newgate Prison in London. No mention is made of prison inspection or visitation with inmates. The report begins by listing six Vices and Immoralities:

1. Personal lewdness of the Keepers and under Officers themselves who often make it their business to corrupt the prisoners, especially the Women

2. Their confederacy with Prisoners in their vices, allowing the men to keep company with the women for money

3. The unlimited use of Wine, Brandy, and other Strong Liquors. . .

4. Swearing, Cursing, Blaspheming, and Gameing

5. Old Criminals corrupting New-comers

6. Neglect of all Religious worships[10]

This list is followed by an outline of proposed reforms to correct each "vice and immorality." Together they offer a glimpse into the way things were.

Corruption was rife among prison staff in the English prisons of the seventeenth century. Inmate consumption of alcoholic beverages was commonplace, as was gambling and all manner of coarse language. Prostitution was facilitated by staff. Female prisoners were regularly used as sexual objects by both inmates and staff. Men and women, juvenile delinquents and seasoned criminals, debtors and murderers—all lived together in the same cramped, shared space. Ventilation was poor and the air reeked. The desperate need for a breath of fresh air was literal as well as spiritual.

The strategies Mr. Shute proposed for addressing prison conditions were varied. They included political action ("procure an Act of Parliament"), networking (appeal to the mayor and sheriffs of London "to use their authority for reforming the Prisons"), mobilization of the faith community ("all good people may be advertised of their abodes and Professions by some publick notice in the Sessions Paper, and exhorted to help them . . ."), and religious education ("That books of devotion be given to all

---

9. Gibson, *John Howard*, 61.

10. Allen and McClure, *Two Hundred Years*, 54.

Prisoners—a Bible to every Chamber").[11] The SPCK was most energetic in employing the strategy of religious education.

Mr. Shute's proposals for reform ranged from enforcement of standards for prison personnel to elimination of alcohol and prostitution for inmates. He proposed separate cells for inmates, or at least separate "apartments" for men and women. Mr. Shute also called for the separation of "New-comers" from hardened criminals who were "Old and Incorrigible." A series of proposals were put forth to rectify "miserably neglected" religious worship.[12]

The proposal that was acted upon was the distribution of religious literature, including "a Bible to every Chamber." The Society began publishing religious tracts to benefit the spiritual life of prisoners. Its work of encouraging members to visit the sick, poor, and imprisoned both motivated and resourced Christian ministry in prisons for years to come. At Oxford, a small group of Anglicans embraced this mission of the SPCK. In due time, they came to be called "Methodists."

THE METHODISTS: "PREACH FAITH"

At the turn of the eighteenth century an Anglican priest by the name of Samuel Wesley corresponded with the SPCK about the founding of a local society in his Epworth parish. He became a member for the remainder of his life. So it is not surprising that his son John took along literature from the SPCK when he went to evangelize native Americans in Georgia.[13]

The mission was a failure and in the years to come neither John nor his brother Charles appear on SPCK membership roles—not so much because of the failed mission, but because their "religious enthusiasm" was found objectionable by the Society. Nevertheless, they and their compatriots at Oxford were influenced by SPCK ideals and practices, and followed in the footsteps of Mr. Shute.

The seedbed of the Methodist movement included ministry with incarcerated persons. The Oxford enthusiasts formed a society modeled after

11. Ibid., 54–57.

12. Ibid., 57.

13. Wesley's correspondence with the SPCK reveals the euro-centric bias that would be typical of Christian missionaries to native peoples in the American, Asian, and African continents, along with outlining what would become standard missionary practice. See Allen and McClure, *Two Hundred Years*, 390–391 for an illuminating letter of complaint.

SPCK local groups with a handful of members. One of them, William Morgan, urged John to visit debtors and condemned felons in a nearby prison. On August 24, 1730 John and Charles joined William at "the Castle."

The experience resulted in agreement that the group would schedule at least weekly visits to the prison. Before the end of the year they also began to visit the Oxford city jail—called "Bocardo"—where two centuries earlier the Protestant martyr Thomas Cramner had been imprisoned for seventeen months.[14] In Wesley's day Bocardo was a holding pen for debtors rather than religious dissidents.

John concluded a letter to his father on Dec. 11, 1730 with a paragraph describing the Methodists' new venue for ministry. He wrote about their fundraising efforts to secure bail for individual prisoners, and their prayers and preaching at the Castle. He concludes: "I had almost forgot to tell you that on Tuesday night Mr. Morgan opened the way for us into Bocardo."[15] The schedule John penned in the front of his diary for the coming year included visits to Bocardo on Monday and Friday, and to the Castle on Tuesday, Thursday, and Saturday. For the next four and a half years he preached at the Castle at least once a month.[16]

By the end of the decade Wesley had moved to Bristol. He developed a charismatic rhetorical style that attracted huge crowds and provoked intense emotional response. He had been in Bristol less than a month when he preached at "the Newgate Gaol . . . a favourite haunt that was open to all comers"[17] (that is, not just to the incarcerated). He records the impact of his preaching:

> One, and another, and another, sunk to the earth. You might see them, dropping on all sides as thunderstruck. One cried aloud. I went and prayed over her, and she received joy in the Holy Ghost. A second falling into the same agony, we turned to her, and received for her also the promise of the Father.[18]

Following the example of the SPCK, Wesley published tracts to resource the expanding Methodist movement. Topics included calls to repentance for persons engaging in various vices and criminal behaviors

14. The trial began on September 12, 1555 and culminated with Cramner being burned at the stake the following spring.

15. Baker, *Works of John Wesley,* 259.

16. Heitzenrater, *Wesley and the Methodists,* 42.

17. Tomkins, *John Wesley: A Biography,* 71.

18. Quoted in Tomkins, *John Wesley: A Biography,* 72.

such as drunkenness, prostitution and smuggling, as well as *A Word to a Condemned Malefactor*. The tracts, like the sermons, were forceful calls to repentance, especially among those condemned to death.

Many crimes, including forgery and theft, were punishable by death. The frequent public executions attracted rowdy crowds who came for sport. The initial attitude of both John and Charles toward deathbed conversions was negative because of the importance they placed on virtuous deeds. They were also skeptical about last minute repentance. Their attitude changed in the wake of John's failed mission to Georgia when they engaged in extended theological discussion with Peter Bohler, a Moravian missionary.

On March 5, 1738, John accepted Bohler's observation that he lacked "saving faith"—faith beyond intellectual assent and works righteousness. He despaired of preaching again. To the contrary, Bohler counseled him: "Preach faith till you have it; and then, because you have it, you will preach faith." The very next day Wesley was able to act on his mentor's counsel in the context of his prison ministry. Meeting with a condemned man in the Castle, for the first time he offered someone salvation by faith alone."[19] It was a pivotal event for John Wesley, for the Methodist movement, and perhaps for the condemned man as well.

In the coming years, as Tomkins reports, "Charles and John continued to carry on an extensive ministry to the prisons, especially Newgate and the Marshalsea in London, the Castle in Oxford, and Newgate in Bristol."[20] Visitation sometimes necessitated perseverance to overcome obstacles. Prison officials could be uncooperative gatekeepers. During the winter of 1943, Charles wrote in his journal about conflict with a "head-jailer" at Newgate prison (London) who repeatedly attempted to thwart Charles' visits:

> [Friday, Jan. 14, 1743] I visited the condemned malefactors in Newgate, and was locked in by the turnkey, not with them, but in the yard. However, I stood upon a bench, and they climbed up to the windows of their cells; so that all could hear my exhortation and prayer.

The Methodists persisted despite opposition, experiencing divine presence and empowerment:

19. Tomkins, *John Wesley: A Biography,* 58.
20. Heitzenrater, *Wesley and the Methodists,* 125.

> [Tuesday, Feb. 1, 1743] Again Townsend refused me admittance; telling me I had forged my order from the Sheriff. Another let me in, with Mr. Piers and Bray. Scarce were we entered the cells, when the power of God fell upon us, first as a spirit of contrition, then of strong faith, and power to exhort and pray.

Perhaps because of their own experience of God's power and grace, this small band of young men had become convinced that God's love and forgiveness is available for all, without conditions or exception.

This conviction was not shared by all those ministering in the jails and prisons. Prison officials were not the only obstacles they faced in their work:

> [Sunday, Feb. 18, 1743] I found the poor souls turned out of the way by Mr. Broughton. He told them, "There was no knowing our sins forgiven; and, if any could expect it, not such wretches as they, but the good people, who had done so and so. As for his part, he had it not himself; therefore it was plain they could not receive it." I spoke strong words to one of them, which the Lord applied, and prayed in fervent faith. I heard the Ordinary read prayers and preach; then spake with them all together in the chapel. All, but one, were brought back to the truth.

The early Methodists worked passionately to save people from the fear of eternal damnation. Theirs was an age when "the everlasting physical torture of damnation and the need to be saved from it were utterly solid realities for ordinary people."[21] Assurance of salvation from such a dreadful fate for those to whom it seemed inevitable was a gift of far greater value than many of us living today would likely appreciate.

Late in life John Wesley met John Howard in Dublin, Ireland, and noted these reflections in his diary: "I had the pleasure of a conversation with Mr. Howard, I think one of the greatest men in Europe. Nothing but the mighty power of God can enable him to go through his difficult and dangerous employment."[22] Two years later Wesley wrote: "Mr. Howard is really an extraordinary man; God has raised him up to be a blessing to many nations."[23] While the Methodists worked to save people from the fear

---

21. Tomkins, *John Wesley: A Biography,* 74.

22. John Wesley, June 21, 1787 journal entry as quoted in Gibson, *John Howard,* 162.

23. Letter from John Wesley to his brother Charles dated June 20, 1789 as quoted in Gibson, *John Howard,* 162–163.

of hell after death, John Howard came along later in the eighteenth century to address the need to save people from hell on earth.

JOHN HOWARD: "THE DISTRESS OF PRISONERS"

A life-long Anglican, John Howard worked for prison reform in the second half of the eighteenth century. It was this work that so impressed Wesley. He was the son of a wealthy upholsterer from London who owned a country estate. He lived the comfortable life of a country gentleman, managing his property, sightseeing in Continental cities and vacationing in English resorts. He married twice; both marriages were happy but short-lived as his wives died. Like his father he was a life-long Dissenter or Congregationalist, a descendant of Puritans.

While committed to this faith tradition and to an evangelical perspective, Howard was a flexible and tolerant Christian. He regularly joined his second wife in worship at her Anglican church and was supportive of the parish. He maintained a rhythm of Bible reading and prayer for private devotions and chastised himself for neglecting his spiritual disciplines. He was a man of integrity who desired to behave in ways becoming a disciple of Christ, "whose mind should be formed in my soul."[24]

Howard was also a man of compassion. He visited those of meager means and treated them with kind attention. He conversed pleasantly with his tenants as well as other poor people in his community. He helped them find employment, provided schools for their children, and constructed new homes so they would have healthy places to live:

> He was a sanitary reformer and an educationalist, in days when neither sanitary reform nor education were of much account. The village of Cardington lies low, and many of the cottages on his estate were damp and unhealthy. Accordingly, new and improved ones were erected, each with a small garden attached.[25]

That these new homes were rented at the same rate as before their rehabilitation testifies to Howard's sense of justice and compassion.

Howard's efforts on behalf of the poor impressed his affluent neighbor Mr. Samuel Whitbread, the lord of the manor at Cardington, who then collaborated with him in these good works. A contemporary described their

24. Gibson, *John Howard*, 21.
25. Ibid., 17–18.

accomplishment: "Cardington, which seemed at one time to contain the abodes of poverty and wretchedness, soon became one of the neatest villages in the kingdom."[26] In years to come John Howard would demonstrate the depth of his compassion and exhort others to exhibit the same. His work for prison reform would be rooted in strong Christian conviction: "We are required to imitate our gracious Heavenly Parent, who is *'kind to the unthankful and the evil.'*"[27] His attitudes and work bore witness to the teachings of Jesus about loving one's enemies and forgiving those who sin against us.

Two experiences of Howard's life before beginning the vocation that made him famous are worthy of mention. Both occurred in his thirtieth year. Shortly after the death of his first wife he traveled to Portugal to tour the country and visit the scene of the great Lisbon earthquake of 1755. His plans were thwarted when a French privateer captured his boat. He was held captive for two months, experiencing first-hand the suffering of imprisonment A note in his book written some twenty years later on *The State of the Prisons in England and Wales* reflects on this experience: "Perhaps what I suffered on this occasion increased my sympathy with the unhappy people whose case is the subject of this book."[28] This reflection bears witness to the ways in which painful life experiences can be used for good and ultimately be redeemed.

About this same time Howard was elected a Fellow of the Royal Society. His contributions to the work of the Society were limited. Nevertheless, they demonstrated a delight in scientific study, ability to engage in objective observation, attention to detail, and an aptitude for statistical collection and analysis. These gifts would be well used in the service of prison reform, a vocation which began for John Howard sixteen years later in 1773 at the age of forty-six.

In that year, Howard was appointed High Sheriff of the County of Bedford. While fulfilling duties as High Sheriff he became aware of the absurd injustice of the English criminal justice system. Rather than accept the status quo, he began a personal crusade which lasted until his death seventeen years later. In his own words, Howard describes the event that launched his memorable vocation:

26. Quoted in Gibson, *John Howard*, 19.
27. Howard, *The State of the Prisons*, 23.
28. Ibid., 23.

The distress of prisoners, of which there are few who have not some imperfect idea, came more immediately under my notice when I was Sheriff of the county of Bedford; and the circumstance which excited me to activity in their behalf was, the seeing some, who by the verdict of juries were declared *not guilty*; some, on whom the grand jury did not find such an appearance of guilt as subjected them to trial; and some, whose prosecutors did not appear against them; after having been confined for months, dragged back to gaol, and locked up again till they should pay *sundry fees* to the gaoler, the clerk of assize, etc.[29]

To correct this absurdity Howard proposed to court authorities that a salary be given the jailer in lieu of fees being collected from inmates. The judge was receptive but requested a precedent to justify a new county expense. So Howard checked out the situation in neighboring counties. To his dismay he discovered the universality of this unjust practice, and "looking into the prisons, I beheld scenes of calamity, which I grew daily more and more anxious to alleviate."[30] He had a new calling.

In order to understand the scope and depth of the problem, Howard visited, examined, studied, analyzed, and documented conditions in the various institutions of incarceration throughout the British Isles: "the Town-Gaols and County-Gaols, the debtors prisons and dungeons, the Bridewells and Houses of Correction." In addition to all the shortcomings noted in Shute's report, and a host of corrupt and corrupting practices perpetuated by the system, Howard discovered and subsequently brought to light horrendous living conditions. These were summarized for an American audience in 1833 by Mrs. John Farrar:

The English prisons were, for the most part, too small for the numbers they contained; they were therefore crowded, and as the windows were very few and very small, the prisoners wanted air as well as room. They were not made secure by being well built, or by having proper walls around them, or proper guards; therefore the prisoners were loaded with irons, to prevent their making their escape. Damp, unwholesome dungeons, many feet under ground, were used as sleeping apartments, and in many places no bed-stead or bedding of any kind was allowed; not even straw was furnished; the damp earth was all the poor creatures had to lie on.

29. Ibid., 1.
30. Ibid., 2.

Very often the prisons and yards were without any drains or sewers to carry off their moisture and filth, and without any wells or pumps within the walls; and so offensive were the cells, dungeons, and even upper apartments of such buildings, that the bad air produced a fever peculiar to prisons, and known by the name of the gaol-fever. This frequently carried off more prisoners in a year than were condemned to death by the law. It spread as rapidly as the yellow fever and was often as fatal.[31]

When this "gaol-fever" spread from the prison into the courtroom and beyond, the public began to pay attention to the need for reform.

John Howard's prison visits extended from England and Wales to Scotland and Ireland. He continued his investigations on the continent, ultimately visiting nearly all the countries of Europe. His goal in visiting these foreign prisons was not primarily to expose abuse; his attitude was one of inquiry rather than condemnation. Consequently, he was rarely denied entrance (the Bastille in Paris being a notable exception). He was searching for ideas to improve things at home before publically disclosing "the horrible state of things which existed in almost every gaol in the kingdom."[32] He commented on the good that he found in people and places. He intentionally looked for light in the darkness, for God in the midst of hell, which is probably how a man with such a tender heart could sustain the face-to-face encounter with the human suffering he witnessed.

In 1774 Howard addressed the House of Commons. The result was passage of an Act of Parliament to address the issue of fees, and a second Act to improve living conditions for the sake of prisoners' health. The passage of laws was an important step, though their significance was more symbolic than pragmatic. Methods of enforcement were not put in place and the new laws were frequently ignored.

The failure to provide for routine inspection by civil authorities guaranteed that no systemic change would be effected. Hence, when Elizabeth Fry entered the common room at Newgate prison she faced the same dreadful setting that Howard had documented. Fry reinvigorated efforts to reform the system, articulated humane principles of crime prevention, paved the way for women's involvement in public life, and alleviated the suffering of countless individuals.

---

31. Farrar, *John Howard*, 57.

32. Gibson, *John Howard*, 50.

ELIZABETH FRY: "REDEEMING THE TIME"

Elizabeth (Betsy) Gurney was born into a large Quaker family of Norwich, England, in 1780. Her father, John Gurney, was a rich man whose wealth came from banking and from the cloth trade that had made Norwich prosperous. Both of her parents were members of the Society of Friends. Her mother, Catherine Bell, brought no dowry to the marriage as her family was poor, but she did bring the status accompanying impressive family relations. Her great-grandfather was the Scotsman, Robert Barclay. Barclay was a theological heavyweight whose writings supported the work of George Fox, founder of the Friends.

Since the founding days of Fox in the mid-seventeenth century there had been a division among the Friends. Those who adhered to strict norms of dress, language, and social behavior were called "plain" Quakers. Those who shed outer signs of religious identity and appropriated norms of the larger culture were called "gay" Quakers. A related category of division was between those influenced by deist theology who maintained Enlightenment ideals of objectivity and rationalism over against those who were "enthusiastic" in their faith.[33] The extended Fry family included both sides of the divide, but her immediate family members were decidedly gay and enlightened. Nevertheless, Christian practices of regular worship, Bible reading, and visiting the poor were part of Betsy's upbringing.

Growing up in the midst of such competing influences, Betsy struggled in her youth to find her own identity. As the daughter of a wealthy gay Quaker, she was expected to participate in high society and practice religious faith with cool detachment. This was not her style. She longed for personal experience of God and for assurance of God's presence and support. She bolstered her confidence to act with supplications such as, "Be with me, O Lord! Then I need not fear what any man or any power can do unto me."[34] She had more in common with the Methodists than with the Anglicans.

The struggle was complicated by gender expectations. As a young woman Betsy was expected to marry, bear children, and manage domestic

---

33. Hatton, *Betsy*, 22. Jean Hatton defines "enthusiasts" as "Christians who were not only openly committed to their faith, but who talked about God as if they had a personal acquaintance with him, preached loudly about it in public and encouraged the conversion of others."

34. Fry and Cresswell, *Memoir*, 223. Journal entry for January 21, 1813.

life. She was expected to eschew public work. But she had a strong sense of calling to work outside the home as well as to public speaking.

Breaking tradition with her immediate family, Betsy donned the cap that symbolized plain Quakerism and entered adulthood with a passionate drive to follow the will of God for her life regardless of how uncomfortable and unconventional the journey might be. Before she was twenty she had established a school for the children of poor families and, with fear and trembling, had spoken at Monthly Meeting. At twenty, she married Joseph Fry.

Drive, faith, and a strong sense of calling sustained Elizabeth Fry through ill health, family conflict, financial disaster, social critique, and nearly a dozen pregnancies as she endeavored to reform prisons and the British criminal justice system. To promote her goals she traveled extensively in Great Britain and continental Europe where she visited prisons, organized visitation groups, preached and networked on behalf of prison reform.

She spoke to thousands, conveying her message of compassion and reform. She met with dukes and duchesses, kings and queens, moving "among the rich and powerful with as much ease as she moved among the prisoners of Newgate."[35] She mobilized family and social connections to raise funds for charitable work and to wield political influence for changing laws.

Along with attending to what happened inside the prisons, Fry also considered the causes of crime as well as the restoration of persons to the community after imprisonment. The goal was "to deter and reclaim the offender."[36] She argued that "the prevention of crime will never be effected by the influence of fear alone,"[37] pointing to poverty, ignorance, and lack of legal options for employment as common culprits.

In reporting on improvements at Newgate prison, *The Fourth Report of the Committee of the Society for the Improvement of Prison Discipline* (1822) credits "the Ladies' Association" (organized and led by Elizabeth) with the result that "there have been many encouraging instances of females, who, on their liberation, have fully proven that the kindness which they have

---

35. Hatton, *Betsy*, 176.

36. "Fourth Report," 14.

37. Ibid., 16.

experienced has not been lost, nor the instruction which has been imparted to them been forgotten."[38]

Fry established procedures that would rival the Methodists in their attention to detail and accountability, as is evident in the committee report:

> For the last twenty months, the Ladies have kept an account of the number of convicted women, who on being placed under their care, were found to have received some degree of education. From this useful register it appears that of 119 prisoners—being the whole number who were able to read—not one had attended a school of the British system . . ."

The value of education for poor and marginalized persons, including those who are incarcerated, was a theme throughout Fry's life. It was an extension of her belief in the value of all people, grounded in her understanding of the Gospel.

In 1827, at age forty-seven, Fry published her own report. It was a book of *Observations on the Visiting, Superintendence, and Government of Female Prisoners.* Only a reading of the full document provides an appreciation of her attention to process and her guiding principles, but chapter titles give an indication of the scope of her work:

> Chapter I: Introductory Remarks [in which she makes the case for women to be active in public good works both as volunteers and as professionals]
>
> Chapter II: On the Formation of Ladies' Committees for Visiting and Superintending Females in Prison
>
> Chapter III: On the Method of Proceeding in a Prison, After the Formation of a Visiting Committee, and on the Proper Deportment of the Visiters [sic]
>
> Chapter IV: On Female Officers in Prisons
>
> Chapter V: On Separate Prisons for Females, and on Inspection and Classification
>
> Chapter VI: On Instruction [academic, pragmatic and religious]
>
> Chapter VII: On Employment
>
> Chapter VIII: On Medical Attendance, Diet, Clothing and Bedding, and Firing [provision for fuel to allow fires during winter for heat]

---

38. Ibid., 42.

Chapter IX: On the Attention Required by Female Criminals on Their Leaving Prison

Chapter X: Conclusion [advocacy for visitation, purposes of imprisonment, objections to capital punishment and public executions][39]

By writing such a book, Elizabeth Fry not only worked for prison reform, but also addressed issues of women's rights.

Fry advanced the status and role of women in more direct ways as well. She organized women's groups wherever she went and advocated for women to be given institutional leadership. She encouraged women to be active outside the home for the good of society. She focused on improving the conditions of incarcerated women, teaching them and giving them useful employment. She ignored discouragement by authorities and other reformers who insisted these women were "unteachable."[40]

Fry's work impacted men as well. This was particularly the case when she moved beyond a focus on conditions to structural change. For example, she worked for systemic change to abolish the death penalty.

Fry's drive was fueled by words she took to heart from mentors she had in her youth. The American Quaker William Savery convinced her at a young age: "There are no lives so unlovely, none so unworthy or so lost, that they are beyond the reach of God's transforming light." Deborah Darby, an English Quaker minister who travelled to America, laid out the promise and the prophecy which guided the young Betsy's future:

> God will visit us all, God who is father to the fatherless and mother to the motherless. You are sick of the world, so you look higher, and you who are to be dedicated to God, will have peace in this world and glory everlasting in the world to come . . . a light to the blind, speech to the dumb and feet to the lame.[41]

These words had a deep impact on Betsy and helped shape the direction of her life's work.

Eighteen-year-old Betsy decided to act on her convictions by "getting together some of the poor children of the district on Sunday evenings and reading Bible stories to them."[42] She began with Billy, teaching in the attic

---

39. Fry, *Observations on Visiting*, Table of Contents.
40. Hatton, *Betsy*, 176.
41. Quoted in Hatton, *Betsy*, 89–90.
42. Pringle, *The Prisoner's Friend*, 46.

of her home, Earlham Hall in Norwich. She planned to increase her student body one by one, but boys and girls came by the dozens until they outgrew their space and moved to the laundry.

Before long Betsy had a class of seventy boys and girls: "the wild, unruly, unwashed children of what were called the lower classes."[43] She affectionately called them her "schollers." Her sisters, impressed that their sibling should be such a successful teacher given that she herself was a mediocre student, called them "Betsy's Imps." Betsy grieved when marriage took her away from her home and her laundry-room school. It is not surprising that her vocation as a prison reformer began with establishing a classroom for the children of incarcerated women.

It happened like this. Stephen Grellet, raised in France as a Roman Catholic, was converted to Quakerism in America by Elizabeth's mentor, Deborah Darby. In 1813 he came to England and visited Newgate prison with two other Quakers. What he saw there distressed him greatly, particularly the women's section:

> The gaoler endeavoured to prevent my going there, representing them as so unruly and desperate a set that they would surely do me some mischief; he had endeavoured in vain to reduce them to order, and said he could not be responsible for what they might do to me, concluding that the very least I might expect was to have my clothes torn off . . .
>
> When I first entered, the foulness of the air was almost insupportable; and everything that is base and depraved was so strongly depicted on the faces of the women who stood crowded before me with looks of effrontery, boldness and wantonness of expression that for a while my soul was greatly dismayed . . .
>
> On going up [to the infirmary] I was astonished beyond description at the mass of woe and misery I beheld. I found many very sick, lying on the bare floor or on some old straw, having very scanty covering over them, though it was cold. There were several children, born in the prison among them, almost naked."[44]

Upon leaving this "abode of wretchedness" Mr. Grellet went directly to the Fry home and unburdened his soul about what he had just witnessed, pleading with Elizabeth that something be done for the children.

She responded by purchasing flannel, recruiting seamstress help, and taking a bundle of clothes for children on the very next day with her friend

43. Ibid., 47.
44. Ibid., 72–73.

Anna Buxton. They, too, were discouraged from entering the women's area. They persisted and found things as described by Mr. Grellet, with nearly three hundred women and many children indiscriminately confined in space designed for less than half that number. The women were dressed in filthy rags, cussing and drinking, receiving their guests with "sneers and defiance."[45]

Elizabeth and Anna gave out the clothing for the children, returning two more times to visit, pray, and distribute clothes. As they knelt and prayed, the women joined them. Elizabeth concluded from these three visits that prison reform "was not only necessary but also possible."[46] However, it would be four years before she would be able to begin her vocation in earnest. In the meantime, she coped with illness, gave birth to her ninth and tenth children, and buried her five-year-old daughter.

In January 1817, at age thirty-seven, Fry returned, alone, to Newgate. Contemporary biographer Jean Hatton describes what happened. Initially the "turnkey" (guard) would not let her in the women's quarters but Elizabeth's will prevailed and she entered by herself. The door was locked behind her. At first there was silence and then derisive laughter, cussing, and a tangible sense of threat. After silently pleading for help she noticed a young woman holding a little girl. Then . . .

> . . . taking the child in her own arms, and laying a hand on the young mother's shoulder, Betsy faced the crowd, "Is there not something we can do for these innocent little children," she asked, "are they to learn to become thieves and worse?"[47]

Fry won the cooperation of the women by gently appealing to their roles as mothers. She shared her own experience and told them a biblical story:

> Pressed upon by their foul-smelling and sweating bodies, and touched by their rags crawling with lice, Betsy told the women that she too was a mother, whose pain when her little daughter died had finally been eased by faith. Presently she spoke of God's passion for sinners and recounted the parable of the vineyard . . . "Jesus," Betsy said, "came especially to save sinners like us." A young woman looked up curiously. "Who is he, madam?" she asked.[48]

45. Ibid., 75.
46. Ibid., 75.
47. Hatton, *Betsy*, 172.
48. Ibid., 172.

After gaining permission from authorities (granted only because they were sure she would fail), Fry identified space in the prison for a classroom. She then recruited an educated inmate to teach, and proved to all that reform was, indeed, possible.

From that time on Elizabeth Fry dedicated her life to caring for the needs of people who were incarcerated. This included basic physical needs like clothing, heat, food, air, bedding, and sanitation. She addressed their emotional and spiritual needs, as illustrated by her visit to Newgate described above. She was concerned about intellectual development:

> They ought to be taught to read, write, and cipher, as well as to make a ready and profitable use of the needle. . .it is most desirable to turn the channel of their thoughts, to improve not only their habits, but their tastes, and, by every possible means, to raise their intellectual and moral, as well as their religious, standard.

Fry advocated that incarcerated persons receive basic education in literate culture skills.

Convinced at the core that no human is beyond redemption, and that society needs to reclaim its wayward citizens rather than to vilify them, Elizabeth Fry was a powerful advocate for reform rather than punishment, for discipline rather than contempt, and for correction rather than revenge. She was not naïve about the effects of crime, nor the propensity of humans to err, so she understood the need for institutions of incarceration. But her approach was one of mercy, not judgment. A letter to her sister captures her spirit as she began her ministry in earnest:

> I have lately been much occupied in forming a school in Newgate, for the children of the poor prisoners, as well as the young criminals, which has brought much peace and satisfaction with it; but my mind has also been deeply affected in attending a poor woman who was executed this morning . . .
>
> This poor creature murdered her baby; and how inexpressibly awful to have her life taken away! The whole affair has been truly afflicting to me; to see what poor mortals may be driven to, through sin and transgression, and how hard the heart becomes, even to the most tender affections.
>
> How should we watch and pray, that we fall not by little and little, and become hardened, and commit greater sins. I had to pray for these poor sinners this morning, and also for the preservation of our household from the evil there is in the world.[49]

49. Extract from letter to her sister, Rachel Gurney, March 24, 1817 quoted in Fry

This work blessed Elizabeth Fry's own life as well as many others. For as challenging, unconventional, and risky as such work was in those days, she was clearly energized by it. It gave her a sense of fulfillment, well-being, and great satisfaction.

Elizabeth Fry understood herself as, in John Wesley's words, "a sinner saved by grace." Aware of her own shortcomings and sins, her own need to pray and read the Bible, and the forces which lead people to wrong-doing, she related to even the most shameful prisoners with humility and respect. This is the reason for the "miraculous effects" that John Randolph observed with such incredulity. The pervasive hope she carried for each incarcerated person was that their prison time would be redemptive. It was the same hope she had for herself and all Christians:

> Earnestly it is to be desired that the number of these valuable labourers in the cause of virtue and humanity may be increased, and that all of us may be made sensible of the infinite importance of redeeming the time, of turning our talents to account, and of becoming the faithful, humble, devoted, followers of a crucified Lord, who went about doing good.[50]

These words come down to us through the years with just as much relevance today in the United States as they had in nineteenth-century England. "Valuable labourers" are desperately needed to challenge the behemoth of mass incarceration.

Like her predecessors—Mr. Shute, John and Charles Wesley, and John Howard—Elizabeth Fry did "redeem the time" given for her life. She engaged in extraordinary works "worthy the attention of angels." Her work provides a solid foundation for Circle of the Word in the Newgates of today. Her spirit inspires courage and conviction to carry out the hard work to which today's disciples are called with regard to visiting in prison and transforming the criminal justice system of the United States.

---

and Cresswell, *Memoir*, 279.

50. Fry, *Observations on Visiting*, 2.

6

The Word of God
in Human Experience

"LISTEN TO THE WORD THAT GOD HAS SPOKEN . . ."

A simple song precedes telling the biblical story in Circle of the Word:

> Listen to the Word that God has spoken
> Listen even if you don't understand
> Listen to the Voice that began Creation
> Listen to the One who is close at hand.[1]

Following a telling of scripture in a worship service at Grace Church, the storyteller announces, "This is the Word of God for all the people of God." Reference to "the Word" is so common in Christian communities that its meaning is unexamined and under-appreciated, though at some level it always seems to refer to something profoundly significant.

But what exactly? What is really being claimed in the song and in the announcement? Exploration of the sources, meanings, and associations of the term "Word of God" in Christian thought and practice uncovers a long and complex history, the conclusion of which is that there is no "exactly" about it. The meaning is almost always ambiguous. Nevertheless, an examination of this history illuminates the potential significance of the biblical

---

1. Adaptation of "Listen to the Word that God Has Spoken," #455 in Eicher, *Glory to God*, music and words anonymous.

storytelling event and why it is appropriate to surround it with references to "the Word of God."

WHAT IS "THE WORD OF GOD"?

A survey of the people on the meaning of the phrase "Word of God" produces quite varied responses. Men in the Horizon Prison Initiative had these associations: righteousness, enlightenment, wisdom, love, hope, Jesus, faith, way of life, intimate conversations, guidance, searching. The director of their program gave this response: "part of God revealed." A woman in a state prison responded, "The Bible." Church members shared their understanding: scripture from the Holy Bible, what God conveys to us with written words. One person offered a list: (1) The Christ (Jesus); (2) God's Spirit within the scripture writers; (3) The read or spoken scripture; (4) God's self-expression; (5) Creator of the world; (6) Giver of light and life; (7) Truth. Another combined several meanings into one statement: "The Word of God created the world and put his Word in the Bible to teach us what to do." These varied responses to an informal survey reflect the complexity of the concept Word of God as used throughout Christian history.

Each response is in continuity with one or another aspect of the faith tradition. A survey of Christian thought also reveals a variety of associations. Trying to follow the line of thought of any given writer is difficult, especially if their writing is taken out of context, because it is often unclear what they are referring to by the phrase "Word of God." Is it the Bible? God? Jesus? Preaching? Efforts to identify the various meanings have been made by both Protestants and Roman Catholics reflecting on this concept in the past century. It is not an easy task, as attested by Walter Ong: "Any understanding of the word of God as word must of course take cognizance of the fact that word of God is used in a number of senses within the Hebrew and the Christian tradition, senses not any the less bewildering because of the fact that all of them are related to one another."[2] This chapter turns to theologians for help in sorting out what is meant by "Word of God" to whatever extent that is possible.

Twentieth-century Protestant theology was deeply influenced by Karl Barth's "Neo-Orthodox" systematic treatment of what he termed the "threefold form" of the Word of God: the Word of God as revealed, written, and preached. The overarching concept guiding Barth's work on Word of

2. Ong, *Presence of the Word*, 182.

God is revelation. He links his understanding to the doctrine of the Trinity. According to Barth, the Word of God, like the Trinity, has a unity such that "we should never regard any of the three forms of the Word of God in isolation."[3] Barth uses preaching and proclamation synonymously, and thereby elevates preaching to a prominent position. Interesting, then, that none of the responses from an informal survey of associations with the Word of God include preaching. Apparently that is not how most people today experience God's Word.

Writing later in the mid-twentieth century, Paul Tillich sorts out six meanings for the "symbol" Word of God. Tillich's perspective is Protestant as well, grounded in existentialist philosophy. He also places his discussion of God's Word in the category of revelation, titling that chapter, "The Reality of Revelation." Tillich sums up his six meanings in one: "God manifest." Tillich's list begins with his concept of God as "the ground of being"—the source and destiny of all "forms." Secondly, Tillich identifies the Word as the "medium" of creation, presumably as depicted in Genesis 1. He describes this approach to creation as preserving the freedom of both the created and the Creator, in contrast to a process of emanation.[4] A third meaning Tillich identifies is "the word received by all those who are in a revelatory correlation," which may be "subpersonal" but is not "irrational." This somewhat esoteric meaning seems to refer to the various ways in which people have experienced divine communication throughout history, for example, as Elijah experienced God in the still, small voice on Mt. Horeb telling him to return to his people and resume his prophetic ministry with them.

Fourth, deriving in particular from the Gospel of John, the Word of God may reference "the name for Jesus as the Christ"—that is, not the historical man, but "the being of the Christ." Fifth, it may refer to a document called the Bible, but not as an exact equation (Word of God = Bible). Tillich laments, "nothing has contributed more to the misinterpretation of the biblical doctrine of the Word than the identification of the Word with the Bible."[5] This suggests a cautionary note in announcing "This is the Word of God" after a scripture reading.

3. Barth, *Church Dogmatics* I.1, 136.

4. "Emanation" is defined by the Miriam-Webster dictionary as "the origination of the world by a series of hierarchically descending radiations from the Godhead through intermediate stages to matter." This cosmogony was articulated in the third century CE by the Neo-Platonic philosopher Plotinus.

5. This observation raises the ante for understanding what is meant when we conclude a scripture telling with the claim, "The Word of God . . ."

The sixth and last meaning of Word of God that Tillich identifies is "the message of the church as proclaimed in her preaching and teaching." Again Tillich is quick to discourage one-to-one correspondence. This does not mean that any given sermon equates with the Word of God. Nor, I would add, does any given telling of scripture equate with the Word of God. Tillich's qualifier is reminiscent of the question Barth posed regarding preaching, "Is there any Word in the words?"[6]

The Jesuit scholar Walter Ong entered the scene on the cusp of the digital revolution in communication technology. In his study of the Word of God in relation to the history of communication, Ong identified eight "main centers of meaning for the term as found in the scriptures and basic church documents from antiquity to the present."[7] Ong uses the language of communication and presence, rather than revelation. His explication is both the most comprehensive and the most lucid of those surveyed.

The first four centers of meaning derive from scriptural analysis, and the second four from historical analysis. According to Ong's scriptural analysis, the Word of God may refer to: (1) an exercise of divine power; (2) communication from God to humans; (3) God's communication to the prophets or others who are to speak for God; (4) the utterance of the prophets or others speaking what God has given them to speak, as from God. Each of these four references is present in the story of Dry Bones (Ezek 37:1–14).

According to Ong's historical analysis, the Word of God may refer to another set of four meanings, bringing the total to eight: (5) what is heard by Christians in sermons; (6) God's communication to the inspired writers of the Bible; (7) what was actually written down in the original texts of the Bible, as well as in all subsequent copies and translations of the Bible; (8) Jesus Christ, as the Second Person of the Trinity, the primary "utterance" of the Father and equally eternal. These eight meanings are reflected in contemporary as well as ancient understanding.

In conclusion, there is no definitive answer to the question, "What is the Word of God?" Rather, there is a constellation of interrelated meanings. The phrase "Word of God" or simply "Word" (with a capital "W") is a multivalent term which signifies some mix of concepts in the mind of those using it. The ambiguity is often appropriate and even intentional. The

6. Karl Barth, *Epistle to the Romans*, 9.

7. Ong includes sources for the meanings he lists. See Ong, *Presence of the Word*, 182–185.

context of its use usually, though not always, helps identify which meaning is intended, whether God the Creator, Christ Jesus, sacred scripture, religious tradition, proclamation, or preaching. So how did this mix arise, and what are some of the problems that arose with it?

THE WORD OF GOD, THE BIBLE, AND CHRISTIAN IDENTITY

It is no great mystery how "Word" as a signifier and as a concept came to be associated with a variety of referents. The canon of Christian faith offers such variety. In the Psalms we have references to the healing power of the Word (for example, Psalm 106). The Psalms also reference both oral and written religious tradition—commandments, decrees, statutes, and ordinances (for example, Psalm 119). The Old Testament begins with an account of creation in which God spoke the cosmos and all its multitudes into being: "God said . . . and it was." God's Word had power and efficacy.

The scriptures go on to record how individuals, beginning with Abram, experienced the Word of the Lord coming to them, telling them things that invariably came to pass, and calling them to work. Often they were told to go someplace, most likely to a place they did not really want to go. Jonah is the quintessential story of this dynamic. The issue for the individual was whether or not God's Word was believed and then whether or not the individual did what that Word commanded; if so it was "reckoned to him as righteousness" (Gen 15:6).

The New Testament records more such stories. According to Luke, Mary is a good example of an individual who heard God's Word, accepted and trusted God's Word, then believed and was blessed by God's Word (Luke 1:26–56). The Gospel of John begins with a hymn which associates Jesus with the pre-existent God, identifying him as "the Word." Acts recounts how Paul is called to teach and proclaim "the word of the Lord" throughout Asia Minor and on to Macedonia.

In the first few centuries of church history, writers like St. Ignatius of Antioch, Origen, and Tertullian considered The Word of God to be "like another, a new, Incarnation or the assumption of a new form by the eternal *Logos*,"[8] whose voice was heard in the Old Testament. They use "Word" to refer to both the Creator and to Christ. These meanings become wedded to written documents in their thinking because, as they believe, "Scripture

8. Bopp, "Salvific Power of the Word," 147.

is the one perfect and harmonious expression of God," and "Scripture is to be understood in this manner, as the uniquely perfect body of the Word."[9] These influential theologians expand the understanding of Word of God from Creator and Christ to a written document.

By the fifth century, the written document—the "Holy Book"—had become an object of great veneration. According to Linus Bopp, "In the time of St. John Chrysostom the Bible was already an object of worship in the Church . . ."[10] This is not surprising since in its infancy Christian identity was closely associated with "the material form of the codex."[11] A codex is a collection of pages bound into a book as is commonplace today.

The ascendancy of the book over the scroll for written communication was a technological innovation concurrent with, and to some extent as a result of, the rise of Christianity. As explained by Horsfield and Asamoah-Gyadu, "One of the elements of Christianity that distinguished it from other religions of the time was not just the content of its texts but also the form in which they were reproduced."[12] Possession of the sacred writings in codex form was associated with persecution for remaining steadfast in the faith, thereby solidifying the bond between the Bible and Christian identity.[13]

When Constantine embraced Christianity and made it the official religion of the Roman Empire he commissioned the production of fifty official copies of the whole Christian scriptures to be placed in select churches. Up until this time (332 CE) what was considered sacred scripture for Christians was in flux and debatable. Constantine's "Bible project" ended the flux and the debate, which would not re-open for another millennium. The Word of God in its written, legal, canonical form was thus established by political authority, as well as by an ecumenical council of the church.

A second consequence of Constantine's Bible project was that the Bible became valued as an artifact, in and of itself, and not just for its contents. It became a matter of prestige to possess a whole Bible. To show it off properly, a Bible would be decorated and placed on display. In a fourth-century

---

9. Ibid., 148. Bopp is citing ancient sources.

10. Ibid., 153.

11. Horsfield and Asamoah-Gyadu, "What Is It About the Book?" 181.

12. Ibid., 181.

13. For accounts of edicts against Christian books under the emperor Diocletian (303 BCE) and the martyrdom of holders of Christian books, see Gamble, *Books and Readers*, 145–48.

sermon,[14] John Chrysostom follows up an observation about the scarcity of books ("games and dice are in most houses; but never books, except in a few") with a lament about the inattention to scriptural content even by those few who owned Bibles:

> I hear no one priding himself because he knows their contents, but because he possesses one written in gold letters. Now, what profit is there in this, pray? The Scriptures were not given merely that we might have them in books, but that we might engrave them on our hearts.[15]

Please note his conviction about the proper place of scripture: engraved on our hearts. Chrysostom seems to have been an early advocate for biblical storytelling.

The significance of the biblical contents was increasingly submerged in the admiration of Bible as artifact as the process of objectification proceeded into the Middle Ages. In worship, there might be much pomp and circumstance surrounding the scripture reading, and especially around the artifact of the book, but little actual engagement by the people with the content of the scripture. Bopp describes the ceremonies with the holy book: "In the processions of the Middle Ages . . . the Gospel book was borne upon a decorated bier."[16] It received more ceremonial dignity than even the Eucharistic elements at that time.

This practice reflected a sacramental view of the Bible—a merging of the understanding of the Word of God as something spiritual with a material artifact. As Michelle Brown summarizes: "Logos, the Word, was the very embodiment of the Creator, revealed to Creation through the incarnation, death and resurrection of Christ and through the abiding physical manifestation of the Gospelbook that contained his teachings . . . That book became, literally, the Word made flesh, or rather, the Word made word."[17]

The Bible as an artifact was so closely associated with the Word of God that many believed it to have divine qualities and powers. Passages of scripture would be carried around the neck like an amulet.[18] Such practices have continued throughout history, especially in communities that

14. Homily 32.

15. *Saint John Chrysostom*, 319.

16. Bopp, "Salvific Power of the Word," 153.

17. Paper by Michelle Brown 2007 quoted in Horsfield and Asamoah-Gyadu, "What Is It About the Book?" 186.

18. Bopp, "Salvific Power of the Word," 153.

are dominated by oral modes of communication. They are present in any communication culture whenever the value of the contents (Word of God) transfers to the container (the book) as a symbol for those contents.

The shift from the Bible as a text of words describing, or even quoting the Word of God, to the Bible as "the collective singular concept of The Word"[19] was also the result of high literate practices. Theological treatments of the text can move so far from the original meaning of the stories that they no longer operate as originally intended. As Horsfield and Asamoah-Gyadu contend, "For Augustine, the Bible is the word of God in material form that has immaterial qualities."[20] It is these immaterial qualities that are most highly valued. The content is theologized through allegorical and other non-literal readings. The stories may be revered as a basis for theological doctrines, but they are not taken seriously as having value in their own right. The original experience reported in scripture is ignored in favor of theological constructs.

This move runs a high risk of leaving the realm of meaning properly attributed to "the Word of God" and doing what Jesus warned against: "You abandon the commandment of God and hold to human tradition" (Mark 7:8). It raises the question of authoritative source, which came to prominence in the sixteenth century. It prompts deeper reflection on the meaning of "Word of God" for the sake of understanding how one is most likely to encounter such a Word, if indeed, as is assumed here, such a Word exists and can be encountered by humans.

AUTHORITATIVE SOURCE: SCRIPTURE, TRADITION, EXPERIENCE

Fierce arguments arose among Christians in the middle of the second millennium with regard to an authoritative source for knowing the Word of God. There were three basic contenders: scripture, tradition, and experience. By "scripture" is meant those preserved writings that were deemed canonical. By "tradition" is meant those practices, beliefs, and doctrines officially approved by high church officials from the days of the early church. By "experience" is meant individual personal experience of hearing God's voice, normally with reference to the Holy Spirit.

---

19. Horsfield and Asamoah-Gyadu, "What Is It About the Book?" 189.
20. Ibid., 189.

Martin Luther, a biblical scholar, initiated the arguments by insisting on the priority of scripture over tradition and claiming that everyone, not just ecclesial leaders, should have access to the Word of God through access to scripture. Before long, others insisted that neither scripture nor tradition was authoritative, only the inner voice of the Holy Spirit.[21] Reformers accused church hierarchy of "shunning" scripture in favor of tradition. Cardinal Robert Bellarmine refuted this accusation in Volume 1 of his *Controversies*:

> The Prophetical [Old Testament] and Apostolical [New Testament] books according to the mind of the Catholic Church, made clear both long ago in the Third Council of Carthage and recently in the Council of Trent, are the true word of God and the certain and stable rule of faith.[22]

Having defended the Church against false accusation, Bellarmine went on to make the case that tradition, as well as scripture, is the Word of God.

In so doing, he differentiated the two by naming the former "the written Word of God" and the latter "the unwritten Word of God."[23] He spells out his argument against Luther's maxim that "Scripture alone is necessary and sufficient for preserving the faith" and carefully articulates why tradition is also necessary. He does not grant the Holy Spirit as experienced by individuals a role in "the total rule of faith" though ultimately all is based on the final authority of God.

The Second Vatican Council (1962–65) emphasized the unity of scripture and tradition, taking a "both/and" approach. It also emphasized the relational aspect of revelation, the role of the Holy Spirit, and the communal fruit of God's Word. Furthermore, it put "extraordinary stress on revelation in Christ.[24] These emphases are reflected in a speech by Pope Francis soon

21. On the Continent, this approach began in a faction of the left wing of the Reformation referred to as the Spiritualists, represented by Casper Schwenckfeld and Sebastian Franck. A century later in England it was fully developed by George Fox, who initiated the Quaker movement.

22. Bellarmine, *Disputations about Controversies*, 6–7. This statement early in the work seems to be contradicted near its conclusion when he writes, "the chief end of Scripture is not to be a rule of faith." However, he will go on to reconcile the two seemingly contradictory statements by calling scripture "a rule of faith, not total but partial."

23. Meaning, as an opponent specified, "unwritten, not because they are absolutely so, but because they were not written into the sacred books by the original authors." See William Whitaker, *A Disputation on Holy Scripture*, 499.

24. Clifford, "The Gift of the Word," 16.

after his election. In April of 2013 Pope Francis had this to say to members of the Pontifical Biblical Commission:

> Sacred Scripture is the written testimony of the divine Word, the canonical memory that attests to the event of Revelation. However, the Word of God preceded the Bible and surpasses it. That is why the center of our faith isn't just a book, but a salvation history and above all a person, Jesus Christ, the Word of God made flesh.[25]

In this statement the pontiff does not use the terminology of "Tradition" to broaden the scope of the Word of God. Rather, he points to Jesus, another referent for Word of God, and one bearing clear scriptural authority.

Most branches of the Reformation, beginning with Luther, also understand the Word of God to be more than a book, in one way or another entailing "the living voice of God."[26] This is not to say that the equation of the scripture with "the eternal Word of God" (meaning, God, the source and destiny of all) has not also been part of Protestant history, nor that current manifestations are absent. Klaus Nürnberger, a Lutheran theologian from South Africa, tells the story of how, in Protestant thought, the scriptures of the Old and New Testaments became equated with the Word of God.[27] This view, as described by Nürnberger, claims that authority rests completely and entirely in the scriptures, which are sufficient in all respects, contain no errors, are entirely clear, and create faith. The scriptures are considered to be identical with the inspired Word of God. Other sources of authority such as oral tradition, Catholic doctrine, and episcopal office are rejected.

The groundwork for this position was laid by a contemporary of Bellarmine, William Whitaker. Whitaker's argument reflects the rising dominance of print communication and the fading prestige of orality that was occasioned by the invention of the printing press. In one instance Whitaker appeals to the pragmatic superiority of print over oral communication: "The scripture therefore is necessary *for certainty*: for those things which are taught orally have not the same firmness and certainty as those which are written and consigned in books . . ."[28] In another place, Whitaker makes the more audacious claim: "God does not teach us now by visions, dreams, revelations, oracles, as of old, but by the scriptures alone."[29] Whether or not

---

25. Richert, "Pope Francis."

26. Nürnberger, *Martin Luther's Message*, 4.

27. Ibid., 87–89.

28. Whitaker, *A Disputation on Holy Scripture,* 499.

29. Ibid., 521.

Whitaker's familiarity with the pedagogy of God is as accurate as he claims remains a question, but he does correctly discern the direction of power with regard to communication systems in his culture.

Taken to its extreme, Whitaker's stance on the Bible as Word of God results in "bibliolatry," where the Bible itself becomes an object of worship. Walter Wink discourages Protestants from falling into this trap by emphasizing, like Luther, the personal nature of God's Word:

> What Jesus gives us is a critique of domination in all its forms, a critique that can be turned on the Bible itself. The Bible thus contains the principles of its own correction. We are freed from bibliolatry, the worship of the Bible. It is restored to its proper place as witness to the Word of God. And that word is a Person, not a book.[30]

From this perspective, it would seem that an embodied telling of scripture, from the heart rather than from the book, would also convey the Word of God.

THE DEEPER MEANING: THEMES

A survey of the current and historical understanding, use, and debates about "Word of God" discloses five principal themes. The first is *Event*. Language about the Word of God involves the language of experience—of happening, occurrence, transaction, and movement through time. "Word of God" does not refer to something static, singular, unchanging, and unmoving. Hence, it is not finally a book. Nor is it a doctrine. It does not refer to pure abstraction or idealized form, nor to information or "deductions made from such 'information.'"[31] It is not an "isolated bearer of meanings"[32]; rather, it is "how we human beings experience God in this world."[33] It is alive and moving through time, though the experience of it may sometimes be so strong that the effect is described as time standing still. There is no appropriate talking about the Word of God that does not involve the language of event.

The second theme names the nature of the event: *Revelation*. "Word of God" refers to God revealing something about God's Self. That something

30. Wink, *Homosexuality and the Bible*, 14.

31. Nürnberger, *Martin Luther's Message*, 12.

32. Ebeling, *Word and Faith*, 313.

33. Hoffman, "Bible as Word of God," 353.

might be a characteristic, an intention, a desire, a command, or a truth.[34] Revelation assumes communication from one to another, in this case from God to humanity. Revelation may be experienced as an unexpected new insight suddenly received, the shedding of light on a conundrum, or a voice delivering a message or telling a story that makes sense of reality.

The days have passed when it can be assumed that all people believe in God and in the possibility of God revealing God's Self. Revelation belongs to the sphere of faith and spiritual experience which finally is a mystery, not a thing to be scientifically proved. Those who do not embrace the possibility of revelation for their lives will not be concerned to engage the Word of God. For those who do embrace this possibility through Christian faith, revelation is experienced not as the result of human speculation about God. Rather, it is experienced as described by Rene Latourelle: "an initiative on the part of the living God who leaves the realm of the mysterious and intervenes in human history."[35] This initiative is revelation.

In the Old Testament "Word of God" refers to divine will as revealed in the Law, through the prophets, and in nature. In the New Testament it also refers to the divine will as revealed in the life, death, and resurrection of Jesus, and to the subsequent work of the Holy Spirit through the community it formed. Many contemporary Christians agree that "God is still speaking"[36]—whether the speaking is labeled "tradition," "inner voice," or "Word." Most Christians affirm that the community of the Church is vital to the understanding of God's on-going revelation.

Orality is a third theme. The means of revelatory communication is first of all oral speech. The spoken word is the most basic way in which humans communicate. Walter Ong's analysis of culture and Christianity from the perspective of communication modes corrects critical misperceptions of literate thinkers: "Today we have often to labor to regain the awareness that the word is still always at root the spoken word. Early man had no such problem: he felt the word, even when written, was primarily an event in sound."[37] Gerhard Ebeling put it bluntly:

> When the Bible speaks of God's Word, then it means here unreservedly word as word—word that as far as its word-character is

34. "Truth" is a dangerous term, frequently abused. It is used here to reference something accurate about reality—accurate for the context, for the time, for the situation.

35. Latourelle, "Revelation, History and Incarnation," 27.

36. "God is still speaking" is a campaign slogan of the United Church of Christ.

37. Ong, *Presence of the Word,* ix.

concerned is completely normal, let us not hesitate to say: natural, oral word taking place between man and man. The Bible can, of course, radically contrast God's Word and man's word, but not in regard to the question of the verbal, or to put it still more sharply, spoken character of the word concerned . . .[38]

From the beginning of the scriptural witness, God is understood to have created all that exists through oral speech: God *said* . . . and it *was*.

Orality happens in time. It is not static and it is not replicable in exact detail. This is because time is always moving, always changing, lived experience. There is no sense in trying to capture a revelatory communication. The Word of God is free to be distinct with each fresh occurrence. On the other hand, the Word of God can be recalled and re-presented with a full complement of "language" that goes beyond "vocables" to include gestures, deeds, and silence.[39] This leads us to a fourth theme.

That theme is personal *presence*. The most basic way in which humans comprehend communication, oral speech, involves one person being present with another and available for interaction. As expressed by Ebeling, "The doctrine of the Word of God is at heart nothing else but the doctrine of God as a Person."[40] This theme not only allows for re-presentation, but also expands the idea of communication to involve all the senses. Abram has visions of the Lord talking to him, even visiting with him at his tent by the oaks of Mamre and there sharing a meal. The prophets, receiving the Word of God, understand God to be with them. And when they are afraid to do what God commands, God promises God's supportive, available presence.

This aspect of "God with us," Emmanuel, is understood by Christians to be fulfilled most completely in Jesus. God communicates God's self, God's Word, via a person who could be heard to speak, but who also could be experienced through all the senses. He touched lepers and little children. He tasted bread and wine. He declined to drink hyssop though it would ease his suffering. Marianne Sawicki describes the Christian concept of presence as intimacy: "Jesus had celebrated a God who wished for new intimacy with men and women, and who established that astounding intimacy in Jesus.

38. Ebeling, *Word and Faith*, 325. Both Ebeling and Ong use "man" to mean "people" as do many of the writers quoted here. At the time they were writing, consciousness had yet been raised to see the harm done humanity by unthinking exclusion of women from the spoken and written record.

39. Funk, *Language, Hermeneutic, and Word*, 13.

40. Ebeling, *Word and Faith*, 352.

The availability of God in Jesus was quite tangible and concrete—as solid, in fact, as a friend sharing food at the dinner table."[41] Presence is the core meaning of the theological concept of incarnation.

Lastly, there is the theme of *power*. The Word of God has creative power to bring into being and to effect response. Beginning with the story of Creation in Genesis 1, the Old Testament attests to this power repeatedly. It also bears witness to the "hardness of heart" that deafens the ear to hear the powerful Word of God, or that fails to trust the Word that is heard. In the Hebrew understanding, Word is connected to breath, to life, to creativity, to the ability to bring something into being or to change that which already exists.

The Greek concept of Word, *Logos*, is different than the Hebrew concept, but no less significant. As explained by Brian McLaren, "For the Greeks, the logos is the internal logic, pattern, or meaning of the universe."[42] Jesus redefined the prevailing Greco-Roman understanding of *kyrios* (lord) from dominance to servitude. So also did he redefine the prevailing understanding of *logos* from a pattern of hierarchical dominance where some had power over others (rich over poor, masters over slaves, men over women), to a pattern generated by the power of love. As McLaren writes, "John audaciously proclaims that the true logic of the universe—the true meaning or syntax or plotline of history—has been enfleshed in Jesus and dwelt among us, full of glory, full of grace and truth, uttering one commandment only: love."[43] The Word that Jesus embodied as one who "was before all things" (John 1:15), ordered those things according to the criteria of love, not dominance.

Tradition and history also bear witness to the power of the Word of God. When people hear the Word, things happen. People experienced the Word and changed allegiances, attitudes, vocations, and lifestyles. Ways and means were created to care for the poor, tend to the marginalized, comfort the bereaved, heal the sick, and school the uneducated. As so clearly seen in the lives of John Howard and Elizabeth Fry, God's Word called some to advocate for the imprisoned. The Word of God, rightly heard and understood, has brought on-going benefits to human community, both to persons who identify themselves as Christian and to those who do not.

41. Sawicki, *The Gospel in History*, 84.

42. McLaren, *Christian Identity in a Multi-faith World*, 141.

43. Ibid., 143.

It is important to engage in discernment when calling something "the Word of God." As Jesus himself noted, much evil has been done by those claiming to prophesy in the Lord's name.[44] Mark Reid identified fifteen criteria for identifying the Word of God today that provide a helpful guide to discernment. One of these criteria he labels "necessary": "The Word of God is *always creative,* never finally destructive. By its very nature it is creative and community building."[45] The power of the Word of God is the creative power of love at work in history, building community.

BIBLICAL STORYTELLING AS WORD OF GOD

In all the discussion of Word of God there is rare mention of the practice of telling the stories of God, out loud and in person.[46] Christianity became so intimately related to literate culture at an early stage in its development, and elevated the book to such high status, that oral presentation of its sacred traditions is not on the radar of most Christian writers. Even though we now know that the early church was formed by oral delivery, we do not take seriously the difference between the experience and impact of written communication and the experience and impact of oral communication.

Oral communication is sometimes valued, but not storytelling forms. Strongly influenced by the Greco-Roman culture in which it developed, patristic Christianity prized classical rhetoric and logical argumentation over storytelling modes of thought. This is ironic since storytelling was the typical mode of thought and teaching in Judean culture, and for Jesus and his first followers. Even when this fact is acknowledged, its relevance for today is rarely noticed.[47]

"Proclamation" is regularly named in connection with the Word of God, and sometimes includes oral recitation of scripture. More often, however, "proclamation" refers to speeches that are theoretically *about* scripture, or at least *based on* scripture. We call these speeches sermons, homilies, or preaching. The scripture-reading/preaching combo are sometimes called

44. See the conclusion to the Sermon on the Mount in Matthew 7:21–23.

45. Reid, "On Identifying the Word," 15.

46. "Stories of God" is here used broadly to reference all biblical contents, not just the narrative genre.

47. In academia, those engaged in the study of the Bible as performance literature are working to correct this oversight. The seminar of the Network of Biblical Storytellers is another venue for exploration of this topic.

"proclamation" and are often treated as forms of the Word of God. Barth uses preaching as a synonym with proclamation, thus raising the sermon to an even higher status than it had already attained in Protestant practice, to a status above scripture. Scripture is read while the Word is preached.

Scripture had long since become a pretext for the sermon. The great evangelical preachers of the eighteenth century such as Jonathon Edwards, John Wesley, and George Whitfield grounded their preaching on a single biblical verse, as had their predecessors. Where the Roman Catholic Church lifted the Eucharist to prominence—a place where God's Word, in one of its meanings, would be experienced—Protestants reserved that place for the sermon. When contemporary worship developed in Protestantism during the late twentieth century, services sometimes dropped the scripture reading completely as a distinctive component of worship, settling for an integration of scripture in the sermon.

A recent description of what typically happens in a mainline Protestant worship service raises an important question: "Some texts are read from the Bible, which takes up a few minutes of time. These are declared to be the "Word of the Lord," but then the preacher spends perhaps five times as long speaking. What, then, is the relationship between the Bible, the word of God, and the sermon? Does the word of God always need such extended explanation or application?"[48]

Yes, explanation of the original understanding of these ancient words is usually needed. And yes, help with connections between the ancient and contemporary experience is usually needed. However, if more attention, time, and energy went into the internalization and re-presentation of the scriptures, a healthier balance would be achieved. The sermon would be strengthened and empowered, and more actual engagement of the Word of God would probably occur.

Common to all understandings of Word of God is the experience of a revelatory event and the personal presence of God, verbal communication, and power that impacts reality. Biblical storytelling draws these components together in ways that are at least as likely to be worthy of the label "Word of God" as the prevailing practices of preaching, scripture lessons, silent reading, and theologizing. Biblical storytelling is an event. It is a living, embodied presentation of material that the faith tradition has deemed revealed.It is oral, and it is powerful. It is often accompanied by a sense of holy power and divine presence.

48. Hoffman, "Bible as Word of God," 353.

The way in which this might happen is eloquently described by Karl Barth in his description of how biblical exegesis can lead to the experience of presence:

> . . . how energetically Calvin, having first established what stands in the text, sets himself to re-think the whole material and to wrestle with it, till the walls which separate the sixteenth century from the first become transparent! Paul speaks, and the man of the sixteenth century hears. The conversation between the original record and the reader moves round the subject-matter, until a distinction between yesterday and today becomes impossible.[49]

If the walls between past and present can become transparent through an experience of the written word, how much more completely might they disappear through an experience of the spoken word. The "text" was originally experienced orally, with all the nuance of meaning and potential of impact made possible by personal delivery. It is fully possible to experience it that way again.

"Biblical storytelling" refers to the act of a person who has internalized a scripture passage and then delivers it in person without a document mediating between teller and hearer.[50] This practice does not seem to have occurred in formal worship since the early days of the church. African American preaching may present an exception. In African American worship, biblical stories are generally read slowly and with gravity. They are then woven into the sermon by the preacher in a powerful, internalized, oral performance. Given the call among both Catholics and Protestants for a revitalization of the Word among us, and the yearning for spiritual meaning in contemporary culture, perhaps it is time for a review and revitalization of this ancient practice of storytelling in all our churches and venues of ministry.

Klaus Nürnberger bases his understanding of the Word of God on Martin Luther's concept of the "living voice of the gospel" (*viva vox Evangelii*): "Christ wrote nothing and spoke everything. The Apostles wrote little and spoke much. The office of the new covenant is not built on tablets of stone that are dead, but on the sound of the living voice."[51] Such an un-

---

49. Barth, *The Epistle to the Romans*, 7.

50. To "internalize" a scripture means to invest time in learning the passage by heart; it means the person has lived with it, studied it, prayed with it, mulled it over, and otherwise engaged it creatively. It is much more than mere memorization.

51. Nürnberger, *Martin Luther's Message*, 4.

derstanding almost shouts for the artistry of a biblical storyteller, though because so few have experienced it, there are few to advocate for it.

Nürnberger understands God's Word from a perspective congruent with twenty-first-century sensibilities as well as with the biblical witness: "The Word of God is the living address of the living God to living people through the words, the fellowship and the behavior of a living community of believers."[52] The Word of God is not just a story told in a vacuum. Nor is its purpose to wage rhetorical war. It is an event occurring both within the covenantal community, and in the covenantal community's witness. It is where the biblical witness is recalled aloud in awareness of the Spirit's active presence for love of God and neighbor. The event includes an invitation to wrap the biblical witness around one's life experiences and share the connections that emerge.

This is where the need and practice of discernment enters the scene. What are the connections between the ancient story and contemporary experience that reflect the intent of the Spirit? What is the Word the Spirit intends to be heard today through the telling and the hearing of the story? The answer involves a quest for "storied knowing," as Lisa Hess names it.[53] In her book *Artisinal Theology* Hess articulates the interplay of divine revelation, story, orality, participatory community, and discernment:

> One could surmise that storying appears to be one of God's ways of self-revelation within history, lived experience, and communities of faith over time. Each generation of the church is faced with the challenge of hearing and telling those stories, the ones that caught the imagination of previous communities of faith, and the ones that the Spirit intends for discipleship today. Discernment is the practice that undergirds the communal awareness and claiming of those stories.[54]

The context for Hess' statement is a discussion of telling one's spiritual autobiography in a small group setting. It is profoundly relevant to the development of a Circle of the Word experience for small groups of incarcerated men or women.

Biblical storytelling is an answer to the pragmatic problem of how God becomes "a present reality or experienced as a power that can make

52. Ibid., 4.

53. Hess, *Artisanal Theology*, 48.

54. Ibid., 49–50.

things happen, when God is accessed through a lifeless text."[55] If the Word of God is ultimately an event of God's revelatory communication, God's personal presence, and God's loving power, then the most direct way of experiencing God's Word may well be through a telling of a biblical story by someone who has studied it, prayed with it, and learned it by heart. This conviction is foundational to every Circle of the Word.

55. Horsfield, "What Is It About the Book?" 178.

7

The Psychology of Hope

In the eighth century BCE, when the Greeks were beginning to write, Hesiod recorded the myth that explained how hope came into the world.[1] According to the myth, Zeus, the king of the gods, did not like people and sought a way to make life difficult for them. So he had a woman created and sent her with a rich dowry to a foolish man named Epimetheus (which means "think later"). She also brought a sealed jar with the words "DO NOT OPEN" written on its neck. The name of the woman was Pandora. Though Epimetheus had been warned never to accept gifts from the gods by his brother Prometheus (which means "think first"), he immediately accepted the jar and opened it. All the troubles of the world flew out. At the bottom of Pandora's jar was one thing more: hope.[2]

Hope is an intangible and essential aspect of human experience, especially in light of all the troubles that accompany life. The lack of hope threatens the well-being of individuals and communities. The narrative of Solomon Northrup about his experience as a Louisiana field slave in the mid-nineteenth century expresses his recollection of teetering on the edge of hopelessness:

---

1. "Myth" derives from the ancient Greek word *muthos* which originally meant "utterance" and came to mean "a spoken or written story." Bellingham, *Introduction to Greek Mythology*, 6.

2. For a version of the story of Pandora's jar, see Bellingham, *Introduction to Greek Mythology*, 21.

> I knew not now whither to look for deliverance. Hopes sprang up
> in my heart only to be crushed and blighted. The summer of my
> life was passing away; I felt I was growing prematurely old; that a
> few years more, and toil, and grief, and the poisonous miasmas
> of the swamps would accomplish their work upon me—would
> consign me to the grave's embrace, to moulder and be forgotten.
> The hope of rescue was the only light that cast a ray of comfort on
> my heart. That was now flickering, faint and low; another breath
> of disappointment would extinguish it altogether, leaving me to
> grope in midnight darkness to the end of life.[3]

Captivity, whether by chattel slavery or criminal conviction, seriously strains the capacity for hope without which life is unbearable.

Many of the biblical scriptures came into being as a hopeful response to experiences of captivity. People experienced God as willing and working for their deliverance from the Egyptians, the Babylonians, the Greeks, and the Romans. In times of distress they remembered and "re-membered," through vivid telling of internalized stories, how God had been present and powerful in the past and had promised good for them in the future. Their part was to place their trust in "the one true God" and demonstrate that trust through obedience to a moral code of behavior. The hope that gave birth to the stories of the biblical tradition and subsequently nurtured the hopefulness of future generations gave people the ability to experience life as meaningful.

The learning and telling of biblical stories, therefore, should be a resource for developing hopeful thinking in jails and prisons. In pursuit of approaches for strengthening the spirit of those who are incarcerated, we will explore in this chapter the concept of hope from the perspective of the social sciences. One of the predominant venues for the scientific study of hope is the field of positive psychology. Therefore, positive psychology will be a starting point for our investigation of hope.

POSITIVE PSYCHOLOGY

In 1954 Abraham Maslow observed that the field of psychology had devoted much more attention to the negatives in human behavior than to the positives. He observed how psychology had much to say about human shortcomings and sins, but little about human potentialities and virtues:

---

3. Northrup, *Twelve Years a Slave*, 235.

"It is as if psychology has voluntarily restricted itself to only half its rightful jurisdiction, the darker, meaner half."[4] The troubles let loose from Pandora's jar drew more attention from psychologists than the antidote for their destructiveness.

Maslow identified the problem and pointed toward a solution. He coined the term "positive psychology" in the concluding chapter of his book on *Motivation and Personality* as a new approach to the study of human behavior. He called for the field of psychology to free itself from the "pessimistic, negative, and limited conception of the full height to which the human being can attain."[5] He encouraged his peers to focus on the positive.

A more sympathetic perspective on the historic bent of psychology toward the negative is that the field has studied human shortcomings for the admirable purpose of helping people who suffer psychological problems. Nevertheless, the call for attention to the positive side of the human psyche was prophetic. An improved understanding of what constitutes and nourishes good living can be helpful to those seeking growth as well as to those seeking more wholesale transformation, as is the case with many in jail or prison.

Individual researchers began to explore aspects of "the good life" through scientific methods. One such pioneer was Rick Snyder, who worked diligently on the topic of hope from the early 1970s. Another pioneer was Martin Seligman, who in 1999 challenged the psychological community to pay more attention to "the good in people and in the world" with the following conviction: "By using the same techniques and tools that help us explain weakness and prevent or treat illness, we could enhance our understanding of strengths and promote well-being."[6] After forty plus years, there was collective follow-up to Maslow's observation. Through networking, collaboration, and advocacy, a positive approach to the scientific study of human experience began.

As a turn of the millennium phenomenon, the field of positive psychology is still in its infancy. Nonetheless, it has already borne fruit through online programs designed to increase optimism and teach children how to be resilient learners. Proponents are confident that continued research will produce further benefits for both children and adults. Unfortunately, as a

4. Maslow, *Motivation and Personality*, 354.

5. Ibid., 353.

6. Lopez and Gallagher, "Case for Positive Psychology," 3.

science, the stature of positive psychology in the academic community has suffered from media coverage that highlights routes to superficial happiness. In the field, this is known as the "hedonic definition" of happiness, having to do with "good moods and pleasurable experiences."[7] It is indeed part of the work of positive psychology, but not exclusively.

To counteract the bad press associated with hedonism, positive psychologists have tended to emphasize the "eudaemonic definition" of happiness. This understanding of happiness is deeper, like the Christian concept of blessing. It has to do with personal growth, meaningful occupation, and connection with others.[8] The value of this focus is evident in works such as *Nonviolent Communication: A Language of Life* by Marshall Rosenberg. This book has resourced people in many contexts around the world. It is currently used as a study guide for incarcerated women in a state prison.

As a Jewish child in urban Detroit, Rosenberg personally experienced the "the darker, meaner half" of humanity through race war between blacks and whites and violent anti-Semitism. These experiences inspired his study of human psychology from the traditional negative manner, asking "What happens to disconnect us from our compassionate nature, leading us to behave violently and exploitatively?" The other question guiding his vocation was, "What allows some people to stay connected to their compassionate nature under even the most trying circumstances?"[9] This exemplifies the eudaemonic focus of positive psychology.

The goal of twenty-first-century positive psychology reaches back to the age-old question addressed in philosophy and religion, "What makes a good life and a good person?"[10] Perhaps by answering this question, it will become more apparent how to help persons who are deemed "bad" by society move toward "goodness" in life and character. A goal of Circle of the Word is to increase the portion of human happiness in the world, or to put it in biblical terms, to cooperate with God's intent that incarcerated men and women can, like Abram, be blessed to be a blessing.[11]

After extensive data collection and analysis across time and cultures, Christopher Peterson and Martin Seligman identified six core virtues or strengths of human life. These are abstract ideals, "encompassing a number

7. Cohn and Fredrickson, "Positive Emotions," 20.

8. Ibid., 20.

9. Rosenberg, *Nonviolent Communication*, 1.

10. Diener, "Positive Psychology, 8.

11. Genesis 12:2.

of other, more specific virtues that reliably converge to the recognizable higher-order category."[12] The following is the listing of the "High Six" as formulated by Peterson and Seligman in their handbook, *Character Strengths and Virtues*:

1. *Wisdom and knowledge*—cognitive strengths that entail the acquisition and use of knowledge

2. *Courage*—emotional strengths that involve the exercise of will to accomplish goals in the face of opposition, external or internal

3. *Humanity*—interpersonal strengths that involve tending and befriending others

4. *Justice*—civic strengths that underlie healthy community life

5. *Temperance*—strengths that protect against excess

6. *Transcendence*—strengths that forge connections to the larger universe and provide meaning[13]

The specific virtues or strengths named in the transcendence category are: appreciation of beauty and excellence, gratitude, hope, humor, and spirituality. Thus, in the positive psychology scheme of character strengths and virtues, hope is located as a transcendent value.

Kant described the transcendent as being "that which is beyond human knowledge."[14] Peterson and Seligman define transcendence as "the connection to something higher—the belief that there is meaning or purpose larger than ourselves." This helps explain why the experience of hopelessness is so closely related to the sense that life has no meaning. A jump from hopelessness is often made to the conviction that life has no value or point. The consequence is often the loss of will to live.[15]

The higher, larger purpose to which a person connects may be of a religious or spiritual nature, but not necessarily. According to Peterson and Seligman it may be "something or someone earthly that inspires awe, hope, or even gratitude—anything that makes our everyday concerns seem

---

12. Peterson and Seligman, *Character Strengths and Virtues*, 35.

13. Ibid., 29–30. Peterson and Seligman list and describe the six core virtues in Table 1.1.

14. Ibid., 38.

15. Existentialists like Camus did not make this jump. Camus presented a case for courage in the face of the absence of transcendent realities and the resulting affirmation of meaninglessness in existence.

trifling and the self seem small."[16] Many things might thereby satisfy the need for transcendence that from a Judeo-Christian perspective would be labeled as idolatry. The relative value of candidates for higher purpose is worth considering in deliberations about ultimate reality. For now it will suffice to note that one of the six core values of human life includes attention to the transcendent as experienced in Christian hope.

It is significant that in this schema, hope is categorized alongside spirituality (with the descriptors religiousness, faith, and purpose) as a transcendent value. The notion of strengthening one's spirit by nurturing hope makes sense in light of this relationship. Conversely, one might nurture hope in order to strengthen the human spirit. Furthermore, attention could also be given to the other transcendent virtues—appreciation of beauty and excellence, gratitude, and humor—and to how they might be encouraged in a program of personal transformation[17] and spiritual empowerment such as Circle of the Word. For now we will focus on hope.

The classification of hope in the positive psychology schema developed by Peterson and Seligman includes further descriptors:

- Optimism, future-mindedness, and future orientation
- Expecting the best in the future and working to achieve it
- Believing that a good future is something that can be brought about

This last descriptor is remarkably similar to that given by an incarcerated man in a brainstorming session on associations of the word "hope." He said, "Hope is looking for a better future." Another man offered this response: "Hope is a belief that something good is about to happen." Hope, then, is a certain orientation to the future.

Sometimes this orientation is toward specific objectives with intentional effort to achieve them. The brainstorming exercise evoked responses such as "striving and focus" and "hope for understanding and forgiveness." In psychological research, hope is often narrowed to a cognitive act that results in certain behaviors, presumably because this is possible to test and quantify. Elsewhere hope is usually understood as having an emotional aspect, something that is *felt* as opposed to simply *known*. Some responses to the brainstorming exercise coupled hope with emotions: "Hope brings joy,"

16. Peterson and Seligman, *Character Strengths and Virtues*, 39.

17. This is a compelling sisterhood of values. Circle of the Word embraces and often sparks humor, playfulness, artistic expression and gratitude, as well as faith and spirituality. It offers a recipe for nurturing transcendent values.

"Hope blossoms into love," Hope is patient endurance." Hope, like biblical storytelling, is experienced in time. It is a dynamic, living thing.

The captive exiles of ancient Israel struggled with hopelessness, as did the disciples hiding behind locked doors and enslaved African Americans like Solomon Northrup. The passage from *Twelve Years a Slave* is a passionate expression of Northrup's feelings regarding the demise of hope. The loss of hope is a common experience of people directly impacted by today's mass incarceration. Living without hope is like living without breath. It is not possible.

POSITIVE EMOTIONS

To the extent that hope is an emotion, and to the extent that hope is beneficial,[18] discussions about the role of positive emotion in a "full and well-lived life" are relevant to the study of hope. Michael Cohn and Barbara Fredrickson provide such discussion in their report on a theory they developed called the "broaden-and-build theory of positive emotions." This theory grew out of their attempt to give positive emotions equal weight as negative ones in shaping a theoretical framework for understanding emotions and their function in human life and culture. The basic claim of the broaden-and-build theory is: "positive emotions 'broaden' people's momentary thought-action repertoires and lead to actions that 'build' enduring personal resources."[19]

In contrast to negative emotions, positive emotions rarely occur in response to life-threatening situations. Incarceration itself may be experienced as life-threatening; the violence common to detention settings certainly is. Negative emotions evoke specific, focused responses such as flight or fight, which are prompted by the emotions of fear or anger. In contrast, according to Cohn and Fredrickson, "positive emotions lead to *broadened* and *more flexible* response tendencies, widening the array of thoughts and actions that come to mind."[20] They offer examples:

> Joy, for instance, creates the urge to play, whether physically, socially, or intellectually. Interest creates the urge to explore, take

18. Sometimes hope is connected with falsity or lack of realism and can be viewed as a negative component of character. The assumption in this chapter is that hope is a positive element of human personality and behavior.

19. Cohn and Fredrickson, "Positive Emotions," 14–15.

20. Ibid., 15.

in new information and experiences, and expand the self in the process. Love—which we view as an amalgam of several positive emotions—creates urges to play with, learn about, and savor our loved ones.[21]

Positive emotions grow a person. They lead to behaviors that expand the horizon of a person's experience and capacity. And they fuel the potential for transformation. The "broadening" aspect leads to a "building" phenomenon.

Broadening enables characteristics to develop that provide a firm foundation for human life to thrive. As Cohen and Fredrickson explain, "Broadened thought-action repertoires did not evolve because of their short-term survival benefits . . . but because of their long-term effects. Broadening 'builds' personal resources." For Cohen and Fredrickson, broadening names "the ways people change while experiencing a positive emotion." Building names "the lasting changes that follow repeated positive emotional experiences over time."[22] Both strengthen a person.

Research has targeted each of these two aspects of the broaden-and-build theory of positive emotions. Results of studies with regard to broadening, detailed by Cohn and Fredrickson, include the following:

- Positive emotions produce patterns of thought that are unusual, flexible, inclusive, creative, and receptive to new information.

- People experiencing positive emotions tend to become more imaginative and attentive regarding things they could do for friends.

- Induced positive emotions can increase trust toward strangers.

- People become less ethnically biased in their face perception and at the same time less perceptive of physical differences between people of different ethnic groups.[23]

Results of studies with regard to the build aspect indicate that:

- Positive emotions contribute to an upward spiral of increasing resources, life successes, and overall fulfillment

---

21. Ibid., 21.

22. Ibid., 15.

23. Results listed here of both the broaden and build hypotheses are quoted from Cohn and Fredrickson in *Oxford Handbook*, 16–19.

- People who experience high levels of positive emotions tend to experience less pain and disability related to chronic health conditions, fight off illness and disease more successfully, and live longer.

- There is an "undo effect" of positive emotions whereby people who are generally resilient against negative events recover more quickly and do so by self-generating positive emotions during the recovery process.

In 2008, Cohen and Frederickson conducted an experiment to test the build hypothesis. It is significant because the results included a wide range of benefits, including an increase in hope. Here is the description of the experiment and its results:

> Participants in the experimental group were trained in loving-kindness meditation . . . which focuses on deliberately generating the positive emotions of compassion and love. After 3 weeks of practice, meditators began reporting higher daily levels of various positive emotions compared to those in the waitlist control group. After 8 weeks, meditators showed increases in a number of personal resources, including physical wellness, agency for achieving important goals [hope], ability to savor positive experiences, and quality of close relationships.[24]

This experiment is also significant because the methods used to attain the described benefits can easily be implemented in a biblical storytelling workshop. A study of the details of this experiment could prove helpful in designing transformative learning experiences through biblical storytelling with people who are incarcerated.

In addition to their own research, Cohn and Fredrickson report on other studies which demonstrate that positive emotions are associated with the ability to take a longer view and develop plans and goals for the future.[25] These abilities are cognitive aspects of hope, as will be explained in the following section on hope theory. Also related to the quality of hope is the impact of positive emotions on people who experience prolonged negative situations like bereavement, joblessness, or incarceration.

Psychological resilience in the face of on-going, negative circumstances is enhanced by some level of positive emotions alongside the unavoidable negative ones. The ability to engage positive emotions even under duress is not a denial of reality, but rather the fruit of acquired emotional

24. Cohn and Fredrickson, "Positive Emotions," 17–18.
25. Ibid., 18.

intelligence. As Cohn and Fredrickson observe, "a broad emotional lexicon makes it possible to find positive moments without denying the seriousness of a negative situation."[26] A broad emotional repertoire avoids the Pollyanna syndrome.

Research on positive emotions has frequently used self-report methods to ascertain emotional states of those participating in various studies. A "Multiple Affect Adjective Check List" was developed for this purpose, but with one hundred thirty-two items included in its list, it has proved too unwieldy for most experimental settings. Consequently, the modified Differential Emotions Scale (mDES) was developed. This scale is more pragmatic with a list of only nineteen items: amusement, anger, awe, compassion, contempt, contentment, disgust, embarrassment, gratitude, hope, joy, interest, love, pride, guilt, sadness, shame, fear, and surprise.[27] Our friend hope is classified as a basic positive emotion.

Other methods for measuring positive emotions have been created to provide more accurate and detailed information than the self-report measures. For example, the use of technology to assess facial responses achieves impressive results: "In *facial electromyography* (facial EMG), electrical sensors placed on the face detect changes in muscle tension."[28] The facial EMG identifies when a person is smiling in a "spontaneous" or "non-posed" manner, even if the smile is too subtle to be observed with the naked eye. Neuroimaging studies of the brain and cardiovascular studies are also informing the empirical exploration of positive emotions.[29]

An interesting aspect of the effort to study positive emotions using scientific methods is the recognition by some researchers of a spiritual dimension of human experience, such as the study that included "loving-kindness meditation." Another utilized "mindfulness meditation." Both of these were variations of guided meditations—a practice often understood as a form of prayer. Several studies aimed at developing effective practices of intervention use counting blessings as a core activity.[30] This common spiritual practice is known as "prayers of thanksgiving" when directed to God.

---

26. Ibid., 18.

27. Ibid., 19.

28. Ibid., 20.

29. Ibid., 19–20.

30. Cohn and Fredrickson, "Positive Emotions," 20.

In a 2006 study, E. M. W. Tong concluded: "distinguishing different positive emotions may require attention to dimensions of experience that researchers have not previously thought of as inherent to emotion, such as social connection and spiritual experience."[31] Tong's proposal is significant, identifying a research void that is needed. The prevailing lack of attention to spiritual or religious experience in research reflects a predisposed opposition to spiritual/religious endemic to academia, according to social scientist Byron Johnson, who advocates research on the relationships between pro-social behavior, criminal behavior, and religion:

> Hostility against faith-based approaches will always exist, but this bias should not prevent people of faith from trying to confront these problems or scholars from studying these efforts.[32]

Let us hope Tong's proposal opens a door to explore a promising area of research.

The ultimate goal of Circle of the Word is transformative learning.[33] Research on positive emotions indicates the possibility of facilitating transformational learning among incarcerated persons through the dynamics of the Circle, since these dynamics elicit positive emotions. After examining this research, Cohn and Fredrickson conclude: "positive emotions help move participants from entrenched habits to new and adaptive ways of acting."[34] Simply put, positive emotions facilitate transformational learning.

When a person is incarcerated they will be required to engage in adaptive attitudes and behaviors to the culture of the correctional institution, many of which may be destructive. These destructive ways of being are added to the set of negative factors that the person has probably already acquired, which resulted in imprisonment. The "entrenched habits" to move away from would be those habits of mind, spirit, and behavior that led to incarceration and which develop as a result of incarceration. The "new and adaptive ways of acting" are those that help inmates heal the wounds of their past, overcome the present dangers of incarceration, and prepare for future success upon re-entry.

Another conclusion is that positive emotions encourage participants to maintain their involvement in a program. Religious programming in

---

31. Ibid., 20.
32. Johnson, *More God, Less Crime*, 10.
33. See Cranton, *Transformative Learning*, for an exposition of this concept.
34. Cohn and Fredrickson, "Positive Emotions," 21

correctional institutions is appropriately voluntary. While one-shot experiences may be the occasion for a life-changing moment, or may plant a seed that bears future fruit, it is much more likely that meaningful growth will occur when a person chooses regular participation in a sustained program. Activities that elicit positive emotions are, therefore, valuable for supporting the goal of transformational learning.

HOPE THEORY

If it is the case that, historically, positive emotions and behaviors have been downplayed by psychiatry, hope as an aspect of human experience has been almost completely ignored. In 1959 Karl Menninger addressed the academy with a lecture on hope because, in his words: "Our shelves hold many books now on the place of *faith* in science and psychiatry, and on the vicissitudes of man's efforts to *love* and to be loved. But when it comes to hope, our shelves are bare. The journals are silent. The Encyclopedia Britannica devotes many columns to the topic of love, and many more to faith. But hope, poor little hope! She is not even listed."[35]

Menninger personally encouraged C. R. Snyder to fill the void. Since conducting a series of studies on excuse-making in the late 1970s and early 1980s, Snyder had been intrigued with the dynamic of hope. Feedback from several participants in his experiments led him to this interest.[36] Following a review of the existing literature, Snyder dedicated himself to pulling together the scattered work that had been done, and networked with interested scholars to further the cause.

In collaboration with students and colleagues at the University of Kansas, Snyder devoted the remainder of his career as a teacher, theoretician, and researcher to the study of hope. His work has been critical to the development of the field of positive psychology in general, as well as to the understanding of hope—its components, dynamics, and significance in human life. Snyder's death in 2006 was mourned by many; his contributions to the field live on in his own work and in the work of those he mentored and inspired.

Snyder's *Handbook of Hope: Theory, Measures, and Applications* includes sections on his theory of hope, on how hope develops and

35. Menninger, "Academic Lecture on Hope," 481.

36. For a discussion of the connection between excuse-making and hope that the studies revealed, see Snyder, "Hypothesis: There Is Hope," 5–6.

deteriorates, on methods for measuring hope, on therapeutic applications of hope theory, and on hope with regard to particular populations (children, elderly people, athletes, survivors of trauma, etc.). Hope with regard to people who are incarcerated does not have a dedicated chapter among the eleven specific groups addressed, but much of the book's content relates to this population.

In contrast to Emily Dickenson's poetic description of hope as "the thing with feathers,"[37] Snyder's definition seems almost painfully mechanical. It is, however, more suited to the needs of social science research: "Hope is the sum of perceived capabilities to produce routes to desired goals, along with the perceived motivation to use those routes."[38] Subsequent definitions were variations on this initial one, all of which focus on three factors: goals, pathways, and agency.

Goals refer to the endpoint of a person's directed efforts. They include achievements to be accomplished (for example, getting a job), states to be experienced (freedom), roles to be embodied (motherhood), or things to be acquired (a house). The goal for Solomon Northrup was rescue from slavery—deliverance. His goal of deliverance was, in Snyder's words, "the anchor" of his hope.[39] Without hope for the goal of deliverance Northrup thought he would, as he writes, "be left to grope in midnight darkness" for the remainder of his life.[40]

Snyder's approach focuses on hopefulness as a thought process more than hope as an emotion, though emotion is clearly connected with thought processes. In a discussion about hope in a Circle of the Word with incarcerated men, one man said, "Hope brings joy." This statement supports Snyder's view: "*emotions are a by-product of goal-directed thought*—positive emotions reflecting perceived success in the pursuit of goals, and negative emotions reflecting perceived failures."[41] Because hope theory focuses on cognition (hopeful *thinking*), it follows that goals must be consciously perceived. Snyder assumes a necessary relation between value and awareness: "Goals need to be of sufficient value to occupy our conscious thought." I am skeptical about the validity of this assumption because I am not convinced

---

37. Published posthumously in *The Complete Poems of Emily Dickinson*. To read the poem, visit http://www.bartleby.com/113/1032.html.

38. Snyder, "Hypothesis: There Is Hope," 8.

39. Ibid., 9.

40. Northrup, *Twelve Years a Slave*, 235.

41. Snyder, "Hypothesis: There Is Hope," 10.

that value directly correlates with awareness, but I do think that conscious awareness of goals is probably necessary for the purposes of experimental research.

A second aspect of the goal factor involves its probability. The chances of reaching a goal are on a continuum from zero percent probability to one hundred percent probability. Snyder points out that neither end of the continuum actually involves hope. As Snyder reports: "research corroborates the contention that people see hope as thriving under conditions of intermediate probability of goal attainment."[42] Something that is one hundred percent probable is just going to happen. It is a *certainty*, not an object of hope. Something that is zero percent probable will not happen, no matter what, and so is also a certainty rather than an object of hope.

The quote from Solomon Northrup's narrative about his experience in slavery takes place following a failed attempt to get rescued. He is saying that his hope for rescue from his perception is nearing the point of zero. He is facing the state of hopelessness, where hope no longer exists. Once he is in fact rescued and reunited with his family, his hope for rescue is also gone because it has happened. He then turns his hope toward the rescue of others by working on the Underground Railroad.

Judgments about the wisdom, or even the sanity, of a particular instance of hopeful thinking involve the degree to which the calculation of certainty is something determined objectively or subjectively. A goal may be completely improbable by objective standards, but nevertheless perceived as a possibility by a given individual. The story of Noah's ark comes to mind. The more improbable the goal, the more ridicule the person will take from peers who judge them foolish, especially if the probability is deemed zero.

But sometimes persistent hope of what seems impossible pays big dividends. For example, there is zero percent objective probability that a person can fly. Flight should not involve hope. Nevertheless, the dream of flight has been around since at least the time of the ancient Greeks. Even in the face of objective impossibility, the goal of flight inspired its attempt by many people for many centuries until finally achieved by Orville and Wilbur Wright of Dayton, Ohio.

This leads to the second factor of hope theory: *pathways*. Pathways or "pathway thoughts" are routes to desired goals. If jumping off a cliff with arms spread like an eagle's wings won't work, try constructing a wing-like

42. Ibid., "Hypothesis: There Is Hope," 9.

structure that attaches to the arms. If that doesn't work, try attaching your-self to a giant kite, or hanging from a silk bag filled with hot air. "High-hope" people try many pathways to arrive at their goal until one finally works, if not for them (folks who try flying by jumping off a cliff rarely survive to try a different approach), then for someone else who builds on their work and on their hope.

When Solomon's first effort to send a letter north explaining his situation and requesting help was sabotaged, he tried again. His first pathway did not achieve the desired goal, but his second pathway did. Many women who attend my Circle of the Word in jail have tried to get free from the heroin addiction that put them there. When one approach to achieving that goal fails, they have hope that another one will succeed.

Along with goals and pathways, the third component of hope as con-ceived by Snyder's hope theory is *agency*. Agency has to do with motivation. It is the energy that drives a person or community toward the goal that is the endpoint of hope. Agency has to do with one's will to achieve a goal, with determination or grit, and with the ability to persevere despite set-backs. The setback Solomon Northrup experienced when he was betrayed by the man to whom he entrusted his letter was excruciating. But, despite the low probability of success and the high cost of failure, he tried again.

Agency has to do with how people respond to the obstacles they en-counter in the pathway to their goal. Do they construct work-arounds? Do they look for another pathway? Do they adapt or alter their goal? Do they "keep on keeping on" or do they give up? What are the resources they bring to bear on the achievement of their goals? These are all factors related to the concept of agency as an aspect of hopeful behavior. They were succinctly summarized by one man in a prison Circle who reflected on hope as involv-ing "striving and focus."

Agency is the aspect of hopeful thinking where Circle of the Word can have tremendous impact. Connection with a compassionate community on the outside, creative engagement with biblical stories, having one's voice in-vited and heard, listening to others' experiences, learning about the stead-fast love of God through the biblical witness—all support the development of agency. Agency is a major dimension of the "spiritual empowerment" purpose for Circle of the Word.

Mary Hallinan organizes and leads a weekly peacemaking circle based on values with women incarcerated at the Montgomery County (Ohio) jail. She affirmed the importance of hope for the women she has come to know in her work there. They had even requested a circle devoted to the theme of hope. The design Hallinan developed was based on the three aspects of hopeful thinking: goals, pathways, and agency. The hope circle was well received and meaningful for the women.

The stories of God's presence and activity in the human community as recorded in the Hebrew and Greek scriptures of the Bible have been a source of hope for many people, especially those experiencing captivity of one kind or another. They have provided transcendent strength for Hebrews enslaved by Egypt, Judeans captured by Babylon, Christians persecuted by Rome, Africans kidnapped to the Americas, and many citizens of many nations who have found themselves behind bars. Then there are all the ways in which individuals and communities are captive to destructive memories and habits of mind, body, and soul who have found hope for deliverance through internalized biblical stories.

And, finally, there is the existential challenge to hope presented by mortality with its certainty of death. This would seem to fit Snyder's definition of a hopeless situation. If avoidance of death is a goal, there is zero percent chance of achieving it. The challenge of death to hopeful living is addressed directly in the Gospels. We are encouraged with Mary to trust an angel's message that "nothing is impossible with God" (Luke 1:37). The learning and telling of biblical stories undergird the core virtue of transcendence by encouraging hope.

8

Circle of the Word in Action

OVERVIEW

IN 2014 I CONDUCTED an action research project with incarcerated men and women that involved hearing, learning, telling, and creatively engaging stories from the biblical tradition as a means of spiritual empowerment. The purpose of this chapter is to provide detailed evaluation of Circle of the Word based on results from this mixed methods study. It includes charts meant to provide graphic presentation of a range of data. These details provide an insight into the impact of the program along with a glimpse inside correctional institutions.

The project investigated the viability and value of internalizing biblical stories as a resource for the spiritual formation of persons who are incarcerated through an interactive small group program structured as a peacemaking circle. The name of the project was "Breath of Fresh Air" and the program was called "Circle of the Word." The primary research question I investigated was whether the internalization of the story of Jesus' passion, death and resurrection through a Circle of the Word format empowered hopeful thinking among incarcerated persons.

The Breath of Fresh Air project was borne out of desire to address the brokenness represented by mass incarceration and to make a positive difference in the lives of those directly impacted by it. This desire was coupled with a hunch about the positive potential of biblical storytelling in detention ministry, specifically with regard to the virtue of hope. The goal of the project was to learn whether or not that hunch reflects reality.

An aspect of this goal was genuine curiosity about how incarcerated individuals would respond to such a program and its specific elements. How would various pedagogical methods be experienced? What improvements would be suggested by participants? Would they choose to participate? Would they recommend the program to others? What benefits would they perceive in participation? I was also interested in learning the extent to which internalizing the specific story of Jesus' passion, death and resurrection would be a source of hope.

I will begin by describing the two institutions where the program was implemented.

CHILLICOTHE CORRECTIONAL INSTITUTION

The Breath of Fresh Air project was implemented in two detention settings. One was a state prison for men in south central Ohio just outside the county seat town of Chillicothe. In 2014 over 20,000 convicted felons were committed to the Ohio state prison system (approximately 17,500 males and 2,800 females).[1] This system is administered by the Ohio Department of Rehabilitation and Corrections. The physical plant of Chillicothe Correctional Institution (CCI) was originally an army base for teaching people to drive Sherman tanks. It was opened as a prison in 1966 on a 72-acre plot. CCI has the most extensive area inside the fence of any Ohio state prison (excluding the farms). Its staff of 540 includes nearly 350 security personnel.

The 2014 prison population of CCI was 2,750. This number includes approximately 875 minimum security inmates, 1740 medium security inmates, and 130 men on Death Row.[2] Of this population approximately one-third are African American. The majority of the remaining two-third's are Euro-American. CCI had the most inmates among Ohio prisons for many years. The introduction of Death Row has moved CCI down to fourth place in total population. According to the Ohio Department of

1. "Ohio Dept. of Rehabilitation and Correction: FAQs," http://www.drc.ohio.gov/web/FAQ.htm.

2. These and other statistics in this section come from "Ohio Department of Rehabilitation and Correction: Chillicothe Correctional Institution," http://www.drc.ohio.gov/Public/cci.htm.

Rehabilitation and Correction, the daily cost per inmate is calculated to be $45.23. In 2014 the CCI website highlighted three distinctive residential programs: the Inmate Reintegration Unit for those who will be released soon, the newly formed Therapeutic Community, and the Horizon Prison Initiative. Breath of Fresh Air was implemented in the Horizon dorm with Horizon participants.

HORIZON PRISON INITIATIVE

The Horizon Prison Initiative is a year-long, voluntary, interfaith program for select inmates. The mission and vision of Horizon is: "to transform prisoners who transform prisons and communities."[3] It grew out of the Kairos three-day spiritual retreat program for people in prison. It is multi-faith, though the majority of participants are Christian. Horizon is a voluntary program accessed through an application and interview screening process. Criteria for selection include a willingness to change, an absence of current disciplinary infractions, and at least two years of a sentence remaining.

Diversity is an important component of Horizon, which accepts participants regardless of faith tradition, age, ethnicity, or crime committed. In the context of diversity, men learn to understand and articulate their own experience and faith commitments more fully, while they are learning to appreciate the life experience and faith traditions of others who differ from them.

During the program, participants live in family units in a dormitory separate from the general prison population. The culture of Horizon is in stark contrast to the overall prison culture as participants learn to get along with former enemies, acquire non-violent conflict management skills, share personal stories, and express emotions. Participants are enabled to address the sources of trauma that contributed to their criminal behavior.

At the time of the project there were Horizon programs at three Ohio institutions for men, with plans for a fourth program to begin at a women's prison. The first one launched at Marion Correctional Institution in 2000; the most recent began at London in 2012. The program in Chillicothe was the largest, accommodating eighty-one men. Its first class entered in 2010. It was staffed with a part-time program coordinator, Richard Boone, who

---

3. Horizon Prison Initiative FAQ, Mission, Vision, Beliefs, Values, and Goals paper, 2014.

is an ordained elder in the United Methodist Church with a Ph.D. in New Testament.

A significant number of volunteers participate as "outside brothers" who journey with a specific inmate throughout his year in Horizon. Other volunteers lead programs under the supervision of the program coordinator. Horizon graduates also lead programs and teach many classes.

Horizon's values and goals are consistent with many aspects of the restorative justice movement. The five core values of Horizon are spirituality, accountability, respect, community, and change. The four stated goals are: (1) to have participants gain a deeper understanding of their chosen faith; (2) to help participants learn to live in a functioning family; (3) to assist participants in contributing to the larger community; and (4) to empower participants to face the reality that brought them to prison. Basic courses taken by all Horizon participants include character reformation, trauma recovery, victim awareness, anger management, and cognitive restructuring.

With a fourteen-year record to examine, it is evident that the Horizon Prison Initiative has made a positive difference in the lives of individuals, correctional institutions, and communities. According to Horizon documentation, "Horizon participants are associated with significantly fewer disciplinary infractions than non-participants."[4] Horizon has also reduced recidivism rates. Program officials estimate a recidivism rate for Horizon graduates that is five times lower than the rate for non-participants.

Despite these positive results, state funding was unexpectedly cut in 2016 and all programs were forced to close except the one in London. This short-sighted budgetary decision driven by political ideology is a sad move in the wrong direction for the well-being of our society.

MONTGOMERY COUNTY JAIL

The other detention setting for the Breath of Fresh Air project was the Montgomery County Jail located in downtown Dayton, Ohio. Maintenance of the jail is the responsibility of the county sheriff. When Dayton was in its infancy 200 years ago, George Newcombe, the first sheriff, met his needs for retaining prisoners by lowering them into a dry well with a rope or by chaining them to a corncrib.[5]

4. Horizon Prison Initiative 2014 brochure.
5. "Montgomery County Sheriff: Jail History/General Info," accessed Oct. 10, 2014, http://www.mcohio.org/sheriff/jail_info.cfm.

As Dayton grew, so did its capacity for housing prisoners. By the mid-nineteenth century the county boasted a jail with limestone walls two feet thick that incarcerated up to seventy people. This facility was replaced by a building equipped with a gallows for public hangings, the last of which occurred in 1877.

The current Montgomery County Jail is the result of renovations completed ten years ago to a facility built in 1965. It has a 914 prisoner-bed capacity. According to the Sheriff's Annual Report, the total number of prisoners booked in 2013 was 27,474 with an average length of stay of twenty days for felons and six days for misdemeanants. Many of these men and women are uneducated, unemployed, and poor, with substance abuse or mental health problems. On any given day there are approximately 800 persons incarcerated in the jail, including 225 women. The project program was offered to women in the jail who were selected by the program coordinator and chaplain, Willie Templeton.

The primary goal of the Montgomery County Jail as stated in the Sheriff's Annual Report is: "to provide a safe and secure environment to promote positive prisoner behavior."[6] According to its website, the jail "has attained the highest honor for observance of national correctional standards."[7] The Report's section on Inmate Programs includes a notice about the project program (at that time called "Life Lessons through the Word"): "In 2013, two new programs were added, *Life Lessons through the Word* and *Spiritual Solutions.*"

Chaplain Templeton screens, coordinates, and trains program leaders and volunteer chaplains. He holds monthly training meetings in addition to a mandated PREA[8] training. His goal as a chaplain and mentor to volunteer chaplains is to bring seeds and water to the persons spending time in the jail.

---

6. "Montgomery County Sheriff's Office Annual Report 2013," accessed Oct. 10, 2014, http://www.mcohio.org/sheriff/ (downloadable PDF),.

7. "Montgomery County Sheriff: Jail History/General Info."

8. Prisoner Rape Elimination Act of 2003. The purpose of PREA training is to insure that the jail environment is safe, humane, and secure, and that inmates are free from the threat of sexual misconduct.

THE PROJECT

In the prison, Circle of the Word was limited to twelve and was fully sub-
scribed. In addition to those twelve, an inmate mentor ("Encourager") participated. He assisted with implementation and data collection. This was a
stable group of men with few absences.

The course consisted of eight sessions over nine weeks. These were
meant to be ninety-minute sessions, but most often were nearly two hours.
Each session dealt with a section of Mark 14–16 in chronological order and
focused on a specific story within that section. The final session included an
"epic telling" of the full narrative by all participants in the course, including
the Encourager and myself. Participants received weekly reading and jour-
naling assignments. Richard Boone was always present in the classroom,
and occasionally interacted with the group.

One-on-one interviews were conducted with each participant before
and after the eight-week "course." Course goals were listed on a syllabus
that was distributed as part of the pre-course interviews. The stated goals
were: (1) Create "a community of reliable others" where each person's voice
can be heard in an atmosphere of mutual respect; (2) Allow the stories to
help us become more fully who God wants us to be; (3) Know one story
well enough to be able to tell it to another person; (4) Gain the personal
power that comes from being firmly grounded in sacred stories. During
the pre-course interview I explained that the course was an action research
project and might result in publication. Confidentiality was assured and an
option not to participate given (which no one took).

In the jail, Circle of the Word was implemented with women. Initially it was called "Circle of the Word" but this caused confusion with the
"Women's Circle" class. Next, Chaplain Templeton named it "Life Lessons
through the Word" but this proved a bit too long. We eventually settled on
"Sacred Stories."

Chaplain Templeton selected participants from those who requested
attendance by sending a "kite." Jail terms are often short, so each weekly
class consisted of new and returning participants. Two other women from
the outside attended each week assisting with Circle leadership, observation, and data collection. They also fully participated in class activities. I
was the primary Circlekeeper.

The same stories from Mark 14–16 were covered in eight sessions. The
series included a ninth session on the story of Jesus' appearance to his disciples Behind Locked Doors from John 20. Sessions lasted ninety minutes,

starting and stopping pretty much on schedule. Chaplain Templeton kept a description of the program in his office in case anyone asked him about it. The description was not publically posted. Women in the jail learn about classes by word-of-mouth.

Since we always had new participants, the research component of Sacred Stories was explained at the beginning of each class. Assurances of confidentiality for participants were also given every week. Survey instruments were offered as an optional activity. The women always completed them, and in fact, expressed disappointment when none were distributed in the ninth session.

The jail proved to be the more challenging of the two correctional settings. One challenge was the unstable class constituency with class membership changing every week. Another was the women's uncertainty about their immediate future. Negative emotions were brought to the Circle: anxiety, depression, anger, sorrow, and frustration. These feelings were obvious from body language, but were also regularly named during the Check-In activity. Also obvious and sometimes named were signs of physical distress. Women suffered from stress, exhaustion, and the ill effects of substance abuse.

"Created a healing circle"

Prior to the action research study, during the fall of 2013, a feasibility study to test the viability of the Circle of the Word process was implemented in the two institutional settings. The goal was to develop a design and try it out before attempting to collect data. A primary reason for this exploratory study was for me to become acquainted with the two contexts. I had very little experience with detention ministry and limited knowledge of correctional settings. I wanted to learn institutional dynamics, establish working relationships with gatekeepers, and gain experience relating to incarcerated individuals.

I designed and led an eight-week series of classes on Mark 1 at both the prison and the jail. Mark 1 was selected for the test program because it is "the beginning of the good news of Jesus, Anointed One" and as such is a good introduction to who Jesus was, what he was about, and the context of his ministry. Mark 1 is also a good introduction to biblical storytelling because the stories introduce basic motifs of the gospel. They are short and compelling. They are also ripe with possible connections to contemporary life experience.

I identified three criteria for a successful pilot program: (1) personal transformation; (2) seed planted to grow in the future; and (3) respite from the pain and stress of the present situation. Feedback indicated these results are possible through a Circle of the Word process. The following is a sampling of responses given by the men during the last class when asked, "What have you achieved?"

- Happiness
- Knowledge
- Bonding as a group—I knew the people but now I have a memory, a shared experience
- Openness, positive energy
- Personal healing breakthroughs, skills for future facilitation
- Personal insight
- Creativity

A survey administered that same day asked the men to write what they would say to others about learning biblical stories by heart. The answers were uniformly positive. Here is a sampling:

- The class is a lot of fun, thought provoking and interesting. I consider myself to have poor memory and was unsure if I would remember any of it, but I have!
- If one is a new Christian, or a child, this would be a great creative and fun way to learn about Christ. If someone is a mature Christian, this will bring the joy and life and simplicity in the Word of God. It is alive!!
- It is a powerful exercise to learn because you can identify with the Bible stories intimately. You are able to express the stories effectively without the Bible.
- This is GREAT, a fun learning experience that you'll look forward to every week. This class will definitely help you to memorize Bible verses and will make you wanna get close to God. Work on yourself. You will enjoy this class, which is also very entertaining. This will benefit you in the long run.

Richard Boone's evaluation was also very positive. It included the following observations about Circle of the Word:

- "An environment where inmates directly encounter the Word of God"
- "The power of God's Word alone touches their heart"
- "A healing circle where strategies allowed for the childlike heart of even the most hardened prisoner to find new life[9]"

Boone's evaluation is significant because of his extensive experience working with incarcerated men.

"This time is like a breath of fresh air"

With a green light from the feasibility study, the project was implemented in the Spring of 2014 with a different group of participants and a different set of stories. A variety of data collection methods were used, both quantitative and qualitative. The data unambiguously shows that participant response to the "Breath of Fresh Air" model was extremely positive.

At the end of Session Six for the men and Session Eight for the women, participants were invited to evaluate their experience of that day's Circle. They rated specific activities as well as overall response. They were asked about their overall enjoyment of the Circle and the degree to which it strengthened their spirit and increased their hopefulness. Both groups indicated high levels of positive response. No one rated their experience in the two lowest brackets. The majority of both men and women rated their experience in the highest bracket. The following charts[10] display these results:

9. These observations were conveyed in a written evaluation sent via email, October 2013.

10. Color coded versions of these charts are available on http://www.circleoftheword.gotell.org.

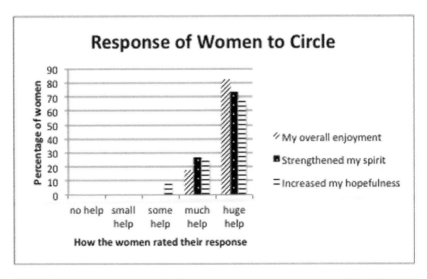

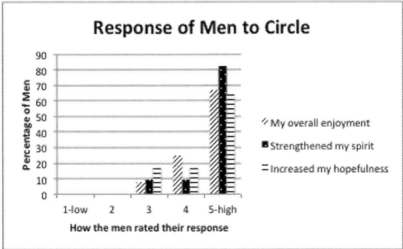

The results of this survey indicate a highly favorable response to the program.

As part of the closing interview following the eight-week program, the men completed a survey designed to help them evaluate their experience of the course. The following charts report the results of that survey for each of nine values. The charts are displayed in the order that the values were listed on the survey.

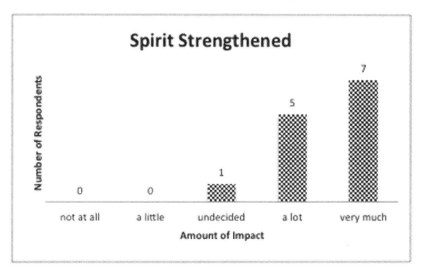

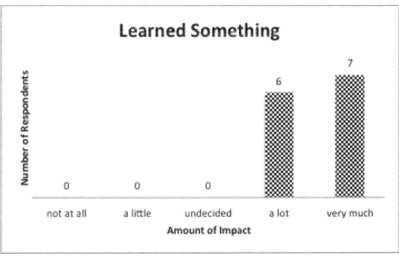

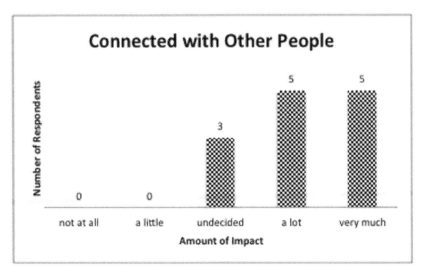

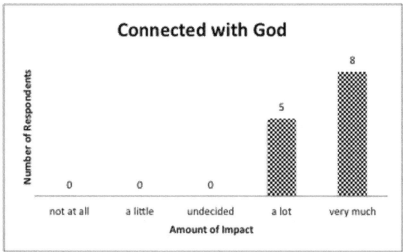

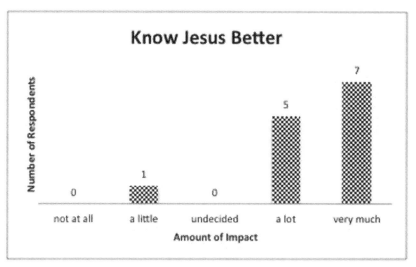

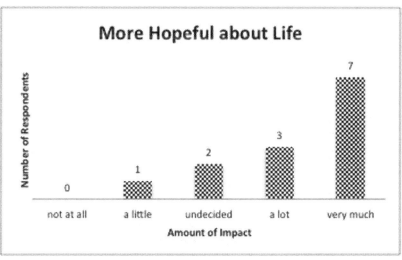

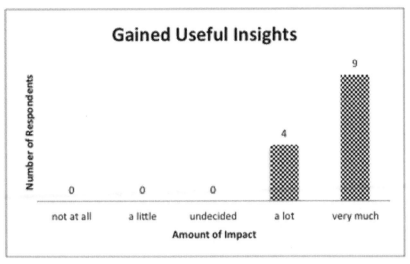

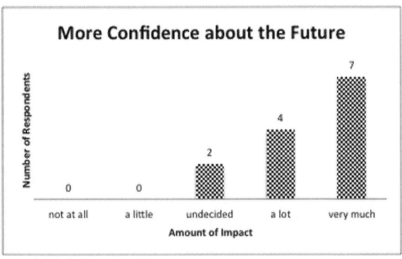

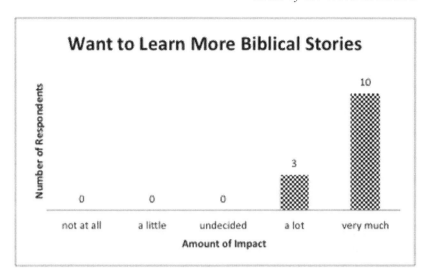

The results of this survey also indicate a highly favorable response to the program. In every category but one, the highest rating was designated by a majority of participants. The sole exception ("connected with other people") evenly distributed the highest and second highest ratings for a majority of favorable replies.

Results of the qualitative data reinforced these positive responses to the program by its participants. Many commented on how it had helped them learn the stories and story details, and how it had given them "tools" to do so. It had motivated them to "get back to the Bible and start reading it again." It was described as fun, entertaining, energetic, interactive, unique, and enlightening.

The men enjoyed and appreciated the amount of time they spent on each story, "taking it slow" and really learning it. They contrasted this approach to previous practice: "When you read the chapter you don't really understand." They observed that this biblical storytelling approach helped them know familiar stories in detail and in depth.

Another named benefit was increasing their "spiritual knowledge" and the way in which the course "helped me understand and connect with the passion of Christ and each person involved in his life." The men also identified a community formation aspect of the program in naming benefits such as:

- Spiritual bonding with the group

- Everyone telling a story

- One body working together toward a common goal led to a sense of unity

- Being in a place with brothers in Christ that I trust enough to open up and share the Word of Christ

- Being able to be a part of this class was a benefit to me

These comments are simple, straightforward witnesses to the sense of belonging which the Circle of the Word course created.

The men gained confidence in their own ability to remember and tell a story. Several men commented on how they had used, or intended to use, what they had learned in the course to tell and teach stories to their children and grandchildren. One said, "I can teach the stories to my twin daughters, in both a serious way and a fun way." A particularly poignant response to the course from one of the men articulated how he perceived the program in relation to hope: "It's a wonderful experience to have, and it allows you to come in touch with the realness of your heart's feelings and desires for your journey in life." Another named benefit related to hopeful thinking: "It helped define my purpose." The responses to the program from the men were varied, meaningful, and positive.

One negative response to the program was reported by Chaplain Templeton of MCJ. He said that one woman felt the Circle activities were too "kindergarten" and while she thought it was okay for others, it was not for her. Going into the project I anticipated this might be a response, especially from the men. I was sensitive to this possibility and concerned about insulting adults who are sometimes treated like children.

For this reason, I did not begin with the Lion Hunt, my customary introduction to biblical storytelling. After a couple of sessions at the prison, the Encourager reprimanded me for omitting this activity which I had done in the feasibility study that he had attended. So the next Circle with the men included the Lion Hunt. It was well received and named as a favorite activity in the closing interviews.

One man called some Circle activities "pre-school." However, this was descriptive, not derogatory, and was said in a context of appreciation. An example of the general attitude was conveyed by the Encourager who said the class was "A must take! Your inner 'child' and inner spiritual man will be enlightened." This recommendation was a strong endorsement from an influential leader.

Women who attended Circle of the Word multiple times expressed their response in comments such as:

- I enjoy coming to this class; everyone is nice
- I've enjoyed this class very much—thanks for coming
- I really like this class, look forward to coming every week
- I'm very thankful for this class
- I love class

Sometimes the women were asked to give feedback at the end of a class. A common report was finding the story meaningful. Many said they were glad to be here. Others mentioned specific activities. One woman's poetic response inspired the project title: "This time is like a breath of fresh air."

The survey that asked the women and men to rate their overall response to a particular Circle also asked about seven activities experienced in Circle that day. The question they were asked with regard to each question was: "How helpful was this activity to you in learning today's story?" The two groups engaged in some of the same activities, while others differed. Below are the results:

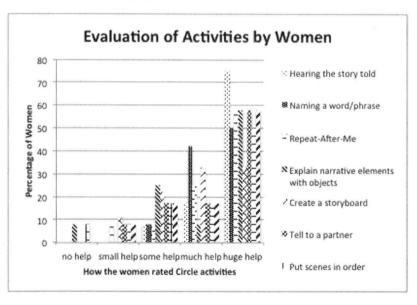

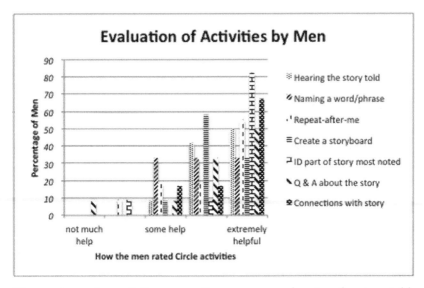

The most popular activity among the women was hearing the story told. The men's favorite activity was their identification of the part of the story that grabbed their attention the most.

In addition to this assessment of response to specific elements of the program for a particular Circle experience, the men completed a more comprehensive survey two weeks after the course. On this survey they rated fourteen elements by circling the face "that best represents your experience." The face icons represented responses ranging from "Didn't work for me at all" to "Worked well for me" as indicated on the survey. Results are displayed in the following two charts:

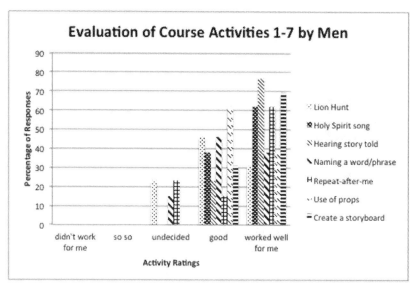

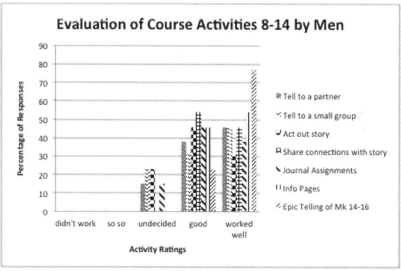

Once again the responses are heavily weighted on the positive side.

It is interesting to note that the two highest ratings were awarded to "Hearing the story told" and "Epic Telling of Mk 14–16." "Hearing the story told" referred to my initial telling of the story as the Opening activity. "Epic Telling of Mk 14–16" referred to the ensemble telling of Mark's passion, death, and resurrection narrative. On the day of the epic telling, one man wrote in his journal:

It was fun. I can't believe we remembered it all to the end. I did not
write in this journal very much. But I loved this class and learned a
lot. I thank you for your time and everything you did for us.

The face-to-face hearing and telling of this central story of the Christian
faith was highly valued by this group of incarcerated men.

Qualitative data emphasized overall enthusiasm for the activities and
pinpointed activities that were particularly appreciated. It did not uncover
any unpopular activity. There was never a sense of resistance to any activity
during a Circle session with either the women or the men. No element of
the program received poor reviews in the concluding interviews.

At the closing of one class at the jail a feedback activity charted what
the women liked about the class and their suggestions for improvement.
The only suggestion they offered was to "have a scribe" to free up the Circlekeeper from this task. This suggestion was implemented for the remainder
of the project. Another suggestion that was made was to give the women
folders for collecting their stories. After securing permission from Chaplain Templeton, this suggestion was also implemented.

Near the beginning of the post-course interview the men were asked
if there was anything problematic about the course from their point of
view. Toward the end of the interview they were asked if there was an element of the course they would have preferred to do "more of" or any they
would have preferred to do "less of." Several men expressed a preference for
more information about the stories and their historical context. Two men
thought there should be more tellings to the whole group (one suggested
an epic telling every week) and two others would like more drawings. One
man suggested more use of the wooden figures and another would have
liked more discussion.

There was always a sense of being rushed in the CCI sessions so the
men were asked for their opinions and suggestions about duration. All but
one man thought more time should be allotted (two hours), but that there
would need to be a break. More movement was suggested to help keep
people alert. One man suggested a morning class to avoid the post-lunch
sleepy syndrome. No one seemed to want to give up any element of the
program. Several wanted more of a number of activities. I took this as a
vote of confidence in the program.

"I want to go to the Sacred Stories class"

Circle of the Word was an elective activity at both the prison and the jail so attendance was a simple way to access inmate response. Taking attendance became an unnecessary task at the prison because nearly everyone came every time. A man who was absent for the second session explained, in a spirit of confession and with apologies, that he had simply forgotten. That was his only absence. The group volunteered explanations of any absence such as, "So and so had a dentist appointment." The Encourager made a point of telling me that if the men didn't find the program meaningful and enjoyable, they would not come. This information negated my previous assumption that the near-perfect attendance was the result of the men feeling obliged to attend once they signed up.

Attendance at the prison remained high even when there were strong forces working against it. During the third session there was suddenly a lot of commotion in the hallway—intermittent cheering which went on throughout the session. My notes tell the story:

> All thirteen men were present and all thirteen stayed for the duration of the class. It was only after we cleared the room that I learned the commotion was cheering during a basketball game between Ohio State University and the University of Dayton. It was a March Madness game of major import for basketball fans in Ohio. On top of that, it was a close game decided in the last four seconds: UD 60, OSU 59. The men in our Circle had missed it without any sign of agitation. They actually seemed less distracted than I was. On reflection, I was very impressed and told them so the next week. We did a round for everyone to name who they wanted to win. One man really didn't care. The others sure did as most of them were from Columbus. I was the only one rooting for the Dayton Flyers.

The men apparently valued their time in what they called "Ms. Amelia's Bible Class."

Another indication that Circle of the Word was considered valuable by participants related to session duration. The men were always fine with continuing class well beyond the norm. Occasionally some had to leave early for their jobs or other commitments. In planning for the feasibility study, the Horizon Coordinator said that classes usually lasted an hour and that the men got restless if they went longer. He was willing to try a longer class session so the test program was designed with ninety-minute sessions and the project program followed suit. The men did not complain about this longer duration. On the contrary, most agreed that two hours would be best as long as there was a short break.

The cap on Circle attendance at both the prison and the jail was twelve. There was one more in the prison because the Encourager functioned as a class participant as well as a mentor to both the men and the researcher. Below is a chart of attendance at the jail:

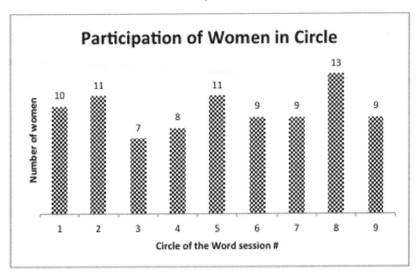

In the jail, attendance in a class is directly related to participant recommendation of that class. Participant recommendation is the only way women find out about programs. It is the only source of publicity. Chaplain Templeton cited attendance as the chief indicator he uses to assess a program's success.

Templeton tracks the data. Women are required to record their presence at the beginning of each class on a form that is returned to him. The following transcript from a post-project interview with Chaplain Templeton narrates these dynamics with regard to the Sacred Stories program:

> I think that the program itself is doing very well. As I've said on numerous occasions, the best advertisement is word of mouth. I can put twenty people in a class, on a class list, and four people show up. Now something's wrong with that picture if that's the consistent thing. But when you have, like for instance your class— I don't put any more than twelve people in your class, so I look for anywhere from eight to ten people on a consistent basis. If I get everybody I'm like wow, yes! But most times I'm not going to

get everybody because somebody may have gotten released, some-body had a visit, any number of reasons come up. Very seldom do I get somebody who refuses: "I don't want to go; I'd rather sit here in a cell." So, I look at Sacred Stories as a success because even during the break I'm still getting kites [messages] asking, "Hey, I wanna go to the Wednesday Bible class; I want to go to the Sacred Stories class."[11]

During the interview, Chaplain Templeton explained that he looks not only at the numbers who attend class, but also at how many women return: "If they go again, that let's us know they like it." We always had women coming multiple times as the following chart shows:

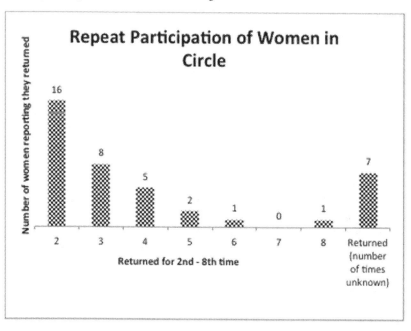

Forty women attended more than once. Since the project, a better method for collecting attendance data has been developed that tracks exactly who comes which weeks. This is now done for the purpose of managing incentives (a certificate for attending four classes; a reward book for attending six), but also continues to document program appreciation.

---

11. Interview with Willie Templeton, Jr. on July 18, 2014.

"The stories give insight"

Feedback during closing interviews at CCI indicated meaningful impact of Circle of the Word on participants through engagement with the stories. In comparing this program to other Bible studies the Encourager commented that while they may listen to the story in other studies they do not get engaged. He said, "There is no talking piece, no chime" and noted that "the drawings are very helpful" for engaging the men. He described a time when two men sought him out to tell him they had seen a TV program that included the scene about Peter's ear being cut off which they had just learned. They spoke with "excitement, energy, life."

One man reported in his journal during the third week about his experience of telling the story to a peer: "I told my story to _____. He told me I did a good job and I had no trouble remembering any of the story. A lot of the story I feel like I can put it in my life." The storytelling was understood not just to be about performance, but about impacting life.

Richard Boone, who works closely with the men as the Horizon Initiative Coordinator, confirmed the high degree of engagement with scripture resulting from the course: "For most of the men this is the most engaged they have ever been with a Bible story. They personally put more into understanding and reflecting on a specific story than they have ever done before." Boone has extensive prison ministry experience. He was present during Circle sessions and was in regular contact with participants outside class. His evaluation is well grounded and significant.

Participants were asked for their opinions about what value the course would have for people who are incarcerated. One participant replied, "If they are sincere it has a lot of value." He went on to elaborate that internalizing the stories this way is the occasion for "a lot of insight—it brings you closer to the scriptures and gives better understanding." He emphasized, "the stories give insight . . . it is just the tip of the iceberg." Speaking of his own experience he said, "It drew my interest" so he thought to himself, "Let me get back in this, see what's going on." He summed up his opinion about the depth of impact by saying, "When the class is over, the class is still going on." And he was not referring to homework assignments.

"It gives me hope"

The virtue of hope was a focus of this project, especially as it related to the stories of Jesus. A survey administered to both the men at CCI and the women at MCJ asked for a rating of the session that day in relation to increased hopefulness. Over sixty percent of both men and women gave the highest rating. One man who gave the highest rating wrote "greatly" next to the category "increased my hopefulness." A man who gave a midpoint rating added an explanatory comment to indicate that this was an increase: "I started the class with zero hope." A survey administered to the men following the course asked for a rating of how much the course had contributed to their feeling more hopeful about their lives. Ten out of the thirteen men gave a positive response with fifty-four percent giving it the highest rating.

There were also unsolicited references to hope. In reflecting on the impact of learning the stories of Jesus' passion, death and resurrection one man said that it renewed hope. Then he went on to elaborate how:

> It renews a hope Knowing his own disciples didn't live up to what they think they should do. It's the same with me. Even though I have [made mistakes] I can still be used in a positive way. [The stories we learned in the course] remind me of that. You forget over time—get worn out, worn down. Hearing it new and fresh definitely renews.

During Check-Out, one woman said she was now feeling, "Hope about eternal life, not only for myself but for everyone." In another session a woman's Check-Out word was "hopeful." The generic "Comments" section on the "Feedback on Class" survey administered to the women at the close of one Circle session elicited this comment: "I was feeling hopeless. Now I am somewhat better." If she were the only one who had that experience, the Circle of the Word model would have proved its worth.

But she would not be the only one. In the years since the "Breath of Fresh Air" project, other women incarcerated at the jail echoed her sentiments. At the closing of a December circle the eleven women in attendance gave feedback on the five-week series called "Journey to Bethlehem." The series had culminated that day with the story of Jesus' birth from Luke 2:1–7. All of the women had attended at least two classes. Two of them specified hope as a result of participation. One said, the class "makes me feel peaceful and hopeful." The other gave particularly interesting feedback: the class "brought me out of my self—it makes me hopeful." According to the categories of core virtues in human life identified by positive psychologists, hope is a sub-category of transcendence. This woman intuited and named the relationship between transcendence ("The class brought me out of my self") and hope ("It makes me hopeful").

Another Circle of the Word series at the jail focused on the stories of Sarah and Hagar. I offered a survey at the end of the class which featured the story of "Sarah's Laughter" from Genesis 18. A twenty-three year old, who described herself as "agnostic/buddhist/wiccan" with "a little experience" of the Bible, indicated that the story was totally new to her, but that by the end of class she could tell it to another person. Her response to "Something I find meaningful about this story" was "It gives me hope."

During the project, there were references to the elements of hopeful thinking, especially with regard to goals. One man at CCI reported with conviction, "It helped define my purpose." Another goal-oriented reflection was given in the closing interview in response to being asked what difference it made in his life to know the story of Jesus' passion, death, and resurrection. This man reported: "Now with incarceration I have strengthened my desire to deal with my spiritual stuff. My issue always revolved around spirituality. I came to deal with my lack of spirituality, 'cause I know if I deal with that it makes me a better person. This course supported that goal. It did that for me."

In response to a question about the impact of learning Mark's story another man spoke of his children and then of his peers in prison: "I got twin daughters. Once you can tell a story to your kids they won't forget it, make it fun. If you can touch your kids, they tell their friends, 'My daddy told me a story.' Individuals in prison—lure them in through your telling so they read—give them hope." This thoughtful man advised a biblical storytelling strategy for imparting hope to incarcerated individuals.

"Different than 98% of what is offered inside the prison"

While the reported experience and program assessment given by the incarcerated participants is critical for evaluating the results of the project, so also are those of the outside participants. This would include the Horizon coordinator, assistant Circlekeepers, and the jail chaplain. All reported positively about the ministry model in post-program interviews.

Chaplain Templeton had this to say about how the program related to his goals as a chaplain:

- I'm concerned about their spiritual well-being. I'm concerned that whatever state they're in when they come in, if they come across my path, whether it be through me personally, or whether it be through you and your class, is that when they leave, they leave better than when they came.

- My goal is that spiritually these folks are well. And that the classes that we offer, the Bible studies we offer, help cultivate, or help feed the inmate to be well, to be better.

- Honestly, I'm extremely pleased with what you guys are doing. I appreciate everything that you guys are doing; the jail appreciates what you are doing.

Chaplain Templeton does not indiscriminately praise or endorse religious programming. He is all too familiar with the potential for leaders to be self righteous or judgmental and for communication to be one-way. His positive assessment of Sacred Stories was not automatic.

Three members of Grace Church assisted with leading Sacred Stories sessions on a rotating basis and evaluated the program within a month after completion. They observed that the women "blossomed during the time" and were "uplifted" by it. They also observed the women's enjoyment and gratitude. Their thoughts about the value and benefits of the program for the women included:

- They learn stories. Some heard, for the first time, of God's love. They perhaps realize that others believe they have value. They get some time when they can interact as people and not prisoners.

- The value to the participants is that they can see God's love at work, they have a chance to listen to and learn stories that may be meaningful to them. They can take part in a variety of learning activities, which can be fun.

These statements are in continuity with Templeton's understanding of that which fosters spiritual growth (and that which does not): "What helps cultivate an inmate's relationship with God is the coming in with a loving heart, sharing the love of God, giving them the truth, but not coming across with an iron fist." The assistant Circlekeepers experienced Circle of the Word as a time when God's love was generously shared and experienced.

Richard Boone's final evaluation of the Breath of Fresh Air project was particularly important because of his extensive experience in prison ministry as an elder in the United Methodist Church, his knowledge of scripture as a New Testament scholar, his Christ-like relationship with the men of Horizon, and his first-hand observation of Circle of the Word over a nine-month period. In many cases Boone's comments find common ground in data gathered from the men themselves. In no case was there a contradiction.

Using the concept of "paradigm shift," Boone described his assessment of how the men had responded to the program: "They sang fun songs they learned in class around the dorm. The fun, maybe even silly things in class, they brought out into the day-to-day life of the Horizon community. They really enjoy this and at some level it is a profound paradigm shift for them. They can live and relate in joy, and not anger and fear."

Boone's listing of values and benefits of the course included confirmation that internalizing the passion, death, and resurrection story increases hope:

- One of the benefits is definitely getting the men to study a passage.

- The story of Jesus' death is now much more personal to them. They can identify with the trial, arrest, and sentencing. They can relate that to their own life experiences.

- They have a positive emotional memory of being engaged with the Bible. For most they even have fun songs and activities they now relate to the Bible.

- They have a place to relate their own experience of suffering to the story of Jesus' death. Their life has more meaning and hope because they now can see how it can relate to Jesus.

Boone also identified how the program supported the four goals of the Horizon Initiative:

- One of the goals of Horizon is to *become a man of faith*. Engaging the sacred scriptures certainly is a foundational spiritual discipline. Also they were brought to a place where they can personally relate the life of Jesus to their own life.

- Second of the goals of Horizon is to *be part of a functioning family*. During the class they were a family. They learned to share at a deep level and receive love.

- Third goal of Horizon is to *deal with the reality of what brought you to prison.* The time they spent reflecting on suffering as it relates to Jesus can be a paradigm shift for them.

- Fourth goal of Horizon is to *contribute to the community.* The invitation to sing, share what they learned with someone else, and to be part of the epic telling helped them see that they can make a contribution to a Christian community.

Boone's discussion of the character of Bible studies and/or spiritual growth classes common in prison settings, and how the Sacred Stories program compares, revealed distinctive characteristics of the Circle of the Word model:

- Most of the religious services in prison are outside groups coming in once and performing. It is one-way communication based on the needs of the outside group.

- There are good Bible study groups. Some of these are driven by a desire to convince the inmates of the correct doctrine of the outside group. Other Bible studies are content driven intended to raise up the level of understanding of the inmates.

- In short there are few places where the needs, thoughts, and desires of the inmates are part of the class sessions. This biblical storytelling had a straight-forward goal of engaging the inmates in a specific story, but it also took them into consideration. What they thought mattered. I would guess that this class is different than 98% of what is offered inside the prison.

It is not only the telling of the sacred story that matters in a Circle of the Word. It is also the telling of personal and communal stories. The healing of memories is facilitated by internalization of the biblical narrative. The data from the Breath of Fresh Air project suggest that this can and has happened through the Circle of the Word process.

"We truly all have value"

None of the three local church Circlekeepers I recruited to help with the project had ever been in a jail or prison before. Nor were they aware of knowing anyone who had been incarcerated. All were apprehensive about what to expect when they first began. They did have experience internal-izing biblical stories, so they knew the potential spiritual benefits of biblical storytelling. In an evaluation meeting following the project, they identified the impact of the program for themselves:

- I was able to interact with the women without judgment that I thought about prior to my first visit. After much prayer to decide to participate in this ministry, I was wrapped in comfort when I came to the jail.

- It was a great life experience learning something about women in jail, how they related to us, to the story, to the other women. I was sur-prised at how articulate and grateful they were. I learned how much we women, of any circumstance, are alike.

- I was surprised by how other-oriented the women were—wanting to help with others' problems even while coping with their own. The laughter was a surprising gift, as well, and I think was healing. I learned that we truly all have value.

All three desired to continue Circle of the Word beyond the scope of the project.

Furthermore, they strongly endorsed this new ministry to become a structural part of their church's ministry. They specified values for the congregation:

- The Bible tells us very directly to visit those in jail. It is a ministry of love, mercy, and teaching so we may be God's instrument in this situation. It helps us overcome feelings of us versus them, to affirm that we are all God's children. Also, it helps us know the importance of reaching out to others.

- It is an encouragement to reach out beyond the church walls.

- It is feeding God's sheep with spiritual and emotional nurture. It is siding with the sheep, and not the goats, and visiting Jesus in jail. It is caring for our sisters in Christ.

It would not be long before these values would be felt by the church.

Within a few months, the vision of the three assistant Circlekeepers actualized into a sustained ministry that continues to grow and impact the congregation. Additional Circlekeepers stepped forward to join the team. The Monday morning prayer group began receiving prayer requests from the women in Circle, written on index cards at the end of class. These are read aloud during the prayer group meeting, and then again by group members throughout the week. Senior Pastor Sherry Gale observes how the prayer cards from the women in Circle of the Word have impacted the prayer group:

> Through the prayer ministry for the women our Grace prayer group has connected with a world outside themselves. This connection has brought a growth in the prayer group participants' understanding and experience of God's love and God's people. The prayer group participants begin to see the commonality of the prayer concerns of God's people from all different life experiences and backgrounds and we experience an amazing unity in our diversity.[12]

In *Redeeming a Prison Society*, Amy Levad advocates relationship between people who are incarcerated and people who are not: "Prisoners ought also to be in communal relationship with people outside of prison, which depends largely upon people outside of prisons venturing into them."[13] Circle of the Word accomplishes this goal. It offers church members the opportunity to grow in discipleship and impact the system of mass incarceration through incarnational relationship with men and women behind bars.

But the processes and spirit of Circle of the Word also accomplish what Levad notices is missing in other religious programs sponsored by outside groups. Circle of the Word assumes the presence and action of the Holy Spirit already in the jails and prisons of America, and allows the outside Circle participants to benefit from that presence and learn from those on the inside. Transformative learning is not limited to incarcerated participants. It extends as a blessing to those of us participating from the outside.

Seeds of Restoration

The Breath of Fresh Air project was designed to explore a hunch that a biblical storytelling workshop using peacemaking circle processes could address the brokenness represented by mass incarceration and make a positive difference in the lives of those directly impacted by it. Results

12. Email communication, December 12, 2014; used with permission.
13. Levad, *Redeeming a Prison Society*, 142.

of project data unambiguously demonstrate that Circle of the Word did make a positive difference in the lives of persons directly impacted by mass incarceration.

But what about the systemic issues? The telling, teaching, and playful enjoyment of biblical stories seem to be an unlikely way to impact the behemoth of mass incarceration in the United States. Does this project really have anything to say about the monster in the closet?

Bryan Stevenson has addressed the ills of mass incarceration by directing the Equal Justice Initiative in Alabama, teaching at New York University Law School, and litigating on behalf of condemned prisoners, the poor, and people of color. In his new book entitled *Just Mercy: A Story of Justice and Redemption*, Stevenson writes, "I have discovered, deep in the hearts of many condemned and incarcerated people, the scattered traces of hope and humanity—seeds of restoration that come to astonishing life when nurtured by very simple interventions."[14]

The Breath of Fresh Air project affirmed the potential for biblical storytelling pedagogy to be one such "simple intervention." It certainly brought positive energy and hope into a particular state prison and a particular county jail.

It is my hope, and my purpose in writing this book, that others will be inspired to bring Circle of the Word to other institutions where incarcerated men and women await a breath of fresh air. The next chapter presents the gist of the program to resource those who might be so inspired.

---

14. Stevenson, *Just Mercy*, 17.

9

Designing Circle of the Word

WHY BIBLICAL STORYTELLING?

THIS CHAPTER IS A how-to chapter written to introduce the basic processes of Circle of the Word so that the potential of biblical storytelling as a means of spiritual empowerment can be tapped for people who are incarcerated. Story is a primary way we make sense of our lives and form meaningful relationships with God and with other people. Those who are incarcerated have broken relationships. Story can help mend them. This dynamic has been validated by the Precious Blood Ministry of Reconciliation in Chicago in their work with youth gang members.[1]

Sacred story helps with the re-formation of memory. The human spirit is formed by weaving one's own unfolding story into the stories of God and God's people. Undernourished or damaged spirits, so prevalent in jails and prisons, can be healed and nourished through connection with biblical stories. Circle of the Word engages people with the Bible for personal transformation.

---

1. To learn about Precious Blood Ministry of Reconciliation and peacemaking circles as a practice of restorative justice visit http://www.pbmr.org/ministries/restorative-justice-community/

PURPOSE

The purpose of Circle of the Word is to provide an opportunity for spiritual growth and reformation of memory through internalization of biblical stories. The goal is an experience of spiritual empowerment. The strategy of internalization, as opposed to memorization, means knowing a story well enough to tell it from the heart because it is part of your own personal story. It also means the ability to tell the story to someone else from start to finish without omitting something of major significance or adding something of major significance.

To tell an internalized biblical story is not necessarily to tell it with word-for-word accuracy, but there should be some interpretive resemblance between the story told and the story recorded in the Bible. Internalization involves knowing something about the original meaning of the story as well as making connections with contemporary life. It is the fruit of repeated hearing and telling, attention to narrative structure and details, and interactive engagement.

The purpose of Circle of the Word is not to learn something in the head that can then be recited as "proof" of some religious doctrine, or even to be more biblically literate. The purpose is spiritual empowerment by establishing connection to the characters of God's story, especially to Jesus, and thus to God. The purpose is ultimately to receive the kingdom of God "as a little child" (Mark 10:15).

Taking Jesus at his word that we are to receive the kingdom of God as a little child, we trust the stories. Trust comes hard for people in prison. If we can help them believe that they can trust God's stories as sources of hope and new life we will have weakened the threat and destructive power of mass incarceration. To receive the kingdom of God as a little child we approach God's stories fresh and with wonder. We engage them creatively, using a variety of learning methods.

PROCESS

A Circle of the Word session combines processes used in biblical story-telling workshops with processes used in the restorative justice practice of peacemaking circles. The peacemaking circle process provides an overall framework for the session by establishing clear guidelines for participation, structuring storylearning activities, and facilitating personal sharing through the use of a talking piece.

Biblical storytelling workshops teach specific stories. Biblical storytelling workshop processes are interactive and creative. A standard workshop has a four-part structure:

1. Learn the story

2. Explore the story in its original context

3. Connect with the story

4. Tell the story

Biblical storytelling workshops often also include "Pray with the story," which focuses on the story as a means of communication between God and people.

BEGINNING

A Circle of the Word session begins by preparing the space. A round tablecloth is placed on the floor, creating the Circle and serving as a focal point for some of the activities. Chairs are rearranged in a single circle around the tablecloth, allowing sufficient room to walk between the chairs and the cloth. On the tablecloth an imitation candle may be placed, along with other objects such as a colorful cloth or the talking piece. Welcoming everyone and introducing Circle leaders is part of preparations. If attendance is taken, this is a good time to do that along with any other administrative tasks.

In accordance with the structure of a peacemaking circle, each Circle of the Word session is framed by an Opening and a Closing activity. These are often similar from week to week. The Opening always includes a telling of the story. Occasionally I have not known the story well enough to tell it. Instead, I do a *Read-Around*.[2] Other components of the Opening include lighting the candle and singing a short song immediately before telling the story. A prayer may be offered after telling the story.

Following the Opening, the use and purpose of the talking piece is explained. The talking piece is an object that is passed from one person to another around the circle to indicate whose turn it is to speak. Once around the Circle is called a "round." Only the person holding the talking piece

2. A description of this activity is available at www.circleoftheword.gotell.org

speaks; all others listen. A person may choose to pass the talking piece on to the next person without speaking. The process is practiced with a Check-In round in which participants say their names and share how they are feeling. They might also be invited to indicate their familiarity with the story and have their responses tallied. Options I give are: (1) brand new to me, (2) somewhat familiar, or (3) I could tell it.

A Circlekeeper—that is, a person facilitating the Circle process—usually goes first in these rounds. By going first the Circlekeeper can model what is to be done. He or she will also be demonstrating vulnerability, which makes it easier for other participants to risk speaking up. Men and women in detention settings are often reticent to speak in a group. They need to feel safe from ridicule, judgment, and critique.

The Circlekeeper explains guidelines for use of the talking piece. The exact form of these may vary. Here are the guidelines I typically use:

1. Honor the talking piece

2. Speak from the heart

3. Listen from the heart

4. Respect confidentiality

A second round provides an opportunity for every participant, including the Circlekeeper, to agree with the Guidelines. The process of agreeing to the Guidelines forms a covenant group—a space where all are invited to have their voices heard and honored. Agreeing to these Guidelines is the only mandatory activity in the Circle. I've never had anyone refuse, though I have occasionally been asked what would happen if someone didn't agree. I respond, "That's never happened but I suppose they would need to leave." This answer satisfies the group; there are murmurs of assent. The Guidelines round completes the first phase of the Circle.

STORYLEARNING

The next phase moves through a series of storylearning exercises. The goal of this phase is for everyone to acquire enough familiarity with the story that they know its characters and basic plot and can tell the gist of the story to one other person without looking at the printed words. I have given these exercises simple, descriptive names. Basic storylearning activities are: *Word I Heard*, *Repeat-After-Me*, *Storyboard*, and *Tell to a Partner*. One or more alternative or supplemental activities might be used, especially with groups that have a significant number of returning participants. They include *Sequence Pictures, Fill in the Blank, The Last Word*, and *Act It Out*. All of these activities are described on the accompanying website: www. circleoftheword.gotell.org.

EXPLORING

"Exploring the story in its original context" encourages participants to gain appreciation for how these stories were understood when they were first experienced by audiences centuries ago. Activities that support this phase often follow the storylearning exercises, but may also be conducted in their midst. The important outcome is honoring the integrity of a biblical story as originally understood before delving too deeply into what we think it means.

The framework for achieving this outcome begins by pointing out that biblical stories are very old, come from a far away place, and were first told in a culture significantly different than our own. We can take advantage of the efforts of historians, archeologists, and biblical scholars to learn about the stories and the people who first told and heard them. Our own understanding will be enriched as a result. Our experience of the stories will have more continuity with the original context than if we only approached them from the perspective of our limited experience and knowledge.

About the Story is the primary activity supporting this component of Circle of the Word. It can be conducted as a mini-lecture, but I prefer to use the *Read-Around* format with a handout. *I Wonder* can also prove helpful, with the added advantage that the questions about original background arise from participants. As with storylearning activities, *About the Story* and *I Wonder* are described on the Circle of the Word website.

CONNECTING

Once everyone has become familiar with the gist of the story and how it would have been understood in its original context, time is devoted to reflecting on contemporary connections. Connections between the biblical story and each participant's personal story are explored. Participants are encouraged to listen for the dynamics of the story in relation to their lived experience. The activity is named *Connections*.

The *Connections* activity is done as one or more rounds. It is for this activity that the talking piece process, with its covenant agreements and option to pass, is most important. The Circlekeeper starts the round with a personal story. While the Circlekeeper talks, others have some time to consider their own connections.

It is still a source of amazement to me how willing both men and women are to voice their joys, pains, and struggles during these rounds. There is something about the biblical stories, and the Circle of the Word manner of engaging them, that elicits meaningful sharing. Connections happen not only between the story and individual participants, but also between participants. As experiences are voiced and honored by attentive listening, community happens. Laughter and tears frequently accompany these rounds. It's a good idea to have a packet of tissues handy.

TELLING

The story is told during all phases of Circle of the Word. Repetition is one of the primary means by which human memory holds onto sensory data. It is also a primary means of influencing one's own story. Best practice is to tell the focus story one last time following the Connections phase. Especially if hard things are shared during that activity, I tell the story again. I introduce the telling by inviting participants to listen with their personal experience in mind. With a gesture of cupped hands, I suggest participants allow their story to be gently held by the biblical story. Sometimes I recommend a way of praying with the story at night. Sometimes we pray right then and there, after the telling.

ENDING

Just as there is an opening ritual that marks the beginning of the Circle, so also there is a standard Closing. Telling the story may begin the Closing. Depending on time and inclinations, it may include activities such as prayer and song. You may wish to do a simple survey for feedback on the Circle or pass out an edible treat (make sure you have permission). Certificates of completion can be awarded. At the prison I issued a certificate upon completion of the eight-week course. At the jail, I give one for every four classes attended.

The end of the session may include an activity I call *Prayer Cards*. I give participants the option of writing prayer requests on index cards. These are taken to the weekly prayer group at Grace Church. Participants can write anonymously since, as we say, "God knows who you are." They could write just their name to be lifted up in prayer. Sometimes they write their own prayers or express gratitude for the prayer group. It may be that someone cannot write and needs to dictate their prayer request.

This *Prayer Cards* activity is a win-win-win for all involved. For those in prison, it provides a source of encouragement and spiritual support. It helps them "not to lose heart" as Jesus taught in his parable of the widow and the unjust judge (Luke 18:1–8). For members of the prayer group it has been a boundary-crossing experience that connects them with a population outside their comfort zone. It provides an opportunity for them to be in prison ministry without being in prison. *Prayer Cards* has also been a gift for those of us who are Circlekeepers. Sometimes all the brokenness shared by participants is hard to bear. It is a blessing to know that neither the participants nor we need to bear it alone.

Before leaving, materials need to be gathered carefully and completely. It is important to be clear about what the inside participants can keep and what must be returned. "Contraband" is always an issue in detention settings. Get clearance with the appropriate officials for anything you plan to bring in and anything you plan to distribute. Participants should be able to keep their copy of the story with their storyboard drawn on the back, along with other handouts such as *About the Story*. Avoid staples in your handouts.

The structure of a peacemaking circle calls for a final Check-Out when current feelings are named, as with the Check-In. Following the Check-Out, our final activity is a send-off song: "Go Now In Peace."[3] The song is accompanied with a few simple American Sign Language signs. It is performed standing in a circle around the tablecloth. Regular responses from participants shift from skepticism, to curiosity, to delight as the signs and the song come together. We offer the blessing of God's peace to one another through the sign expressing "you." The words have special meaning for people living behind locked doors.

3. Words and music by Natalie Sleeth. This short song is available online and in many hymnals. The signs are demonstrated on the Circle of the Word site: www.circleoftheword.gotell.org.

SAMPLE SCRIPT

The sample script below exemplifies the flow of a typical Circle of the Word. This particular script is for a session focused on the story Behind Locked Doors (John 21:19–23). In the design, the words printed in regular style are brief explanations of what to do. The words printed in italics explain what to say. This is a *sample* script, meant as a model and not as a mandate. Take it as a starting place for developing your own design based on your context, gifts, and preferences.

Resources available at a companion website will complete what you need to implement this particular model of Circle of the Word. Located there are:

- Descriptions of each component in the Behind Locked Doors sample design
- Instructions on how to lead various storylearning activities
- PDF files for the charts and handouts
- Resources for a growing collection of Circle designs
- Accounts of my experiences leading Circle of the Word with women in jail

The URL for the Circle of the Word site is *www.circleoftheword.gotell.org*.

Getting Started

Introductions

Set up circle and pocket chart.

Introduce Circlekeepers (names and church affiliation), class (state its purpose), and theme of current story series; review last week's story.

Pass out bags with nametag materials; participants make nametags.

Attendance

Greet participants, take attendance, distribute folders and brochures to first-timers.

Opening: The Story

Light candle, sing "Listen to the Word," tell story, pray.

Explain the Talking Piece

We'll do different activities to learn this story.

Sometimes we'll use a talking piece.

The talking piece creates a space in which everyone can speak and listen in peace.

Each person in the circle gets a chance to speak without being interrupted, and to listen without needing to respond.

When we are using a talking piece, here is how it works:

1. *The talking piece is passed around the circle from person to person.*

2. *Only the person holding the talking piece should speak.*

3. *It is always okay to pass; just say, "I pass."*

Check-In Round

Today our talking piece is a wooden figure of Jesus.

We will use it for a Check-In round. when the talking piece comes to you . . .

1. *Say your name*

2. *Tell how familiar you are with this story (new, heard before, could tell)*

3. *Share a word or more about how you are feeling today*

I'll go first . . .

Guidelines

These are the four guidelines for our time together:

1. *Honor the talking piece—when it is being used, speak only when you are holding it.*

2. *Speak from the heart—tell your truth as you are comfortable to share.*

3. *Listen from the heart—be attentive, with a positive spirit; avoid side conversations, comments or questions.*

4. *Protect personal privacy—Tell about God, Jesus, this class and the story we learn, but keep confidential personal information that is shared.*

Now let us see if we can all accept these guidelines.

When the talking piece comes to you, indicate your acceptance by saying, "I accept these guidelines."

Start a round for everyone to accept the four guidelines.

Engaging the Story

Word I Heard

Listen again to the story of Behind Locked Doors.

This time close your eyes or focus on the candle.

As you listen, notice if any word or phrase gets your attention . . . Read or tell story

Before you open your eyes, think of a word or phrase from the story that got your attention, or another word or phrase that comes to mind . . .

Ring chime . . . *Now open your eyes.*

For this round, name a word or phrase that you heard in the story, or that came to mind in response to hearing the story.

Repeat-After-Me

The most ancient form of education was to repeat the words of whatever was being learned.

So, I'll say a line and then you repeat after me. You can repeat my gestures, too; it will help you learn the story. Here we go . . .

Tell the story in breath units—a phrase at a time—using gestures that connect with the action of the story. Exaggerate words and gestures.

About the Story

Distribute "About the Story" handouts.

Using the talking piece, do a round for reading through the handout, one paragraph per person.

If someone does not choose to read, they can simply pass the talking piece on to the next person.

Storyboard

It's easier to learn a story if you break it down into episodes or parts.

Just like pre-production work in movie-making, we are going to create storyboards for this story to help us learn it.

This story has three parts, so divide your paper into three sections.

I'll tell the story one part at a time. Close your eyes or focus on the candle and see what is happening in your mind's eye as I tell the story.

Now open your eyes, and in the first section of your paper draw a picture of what you saw as you listened to the first part of the story.

Repeat for other parts.

Tell to a Partner

Instruct participants to pair up with a partner and take turns telling the story to their partner using their storyboard to help them remember. No peeking at the other side until both partners have told the story.

When both partners have told what they remember of the story, they check the script and evaluate what they remembered, left out, and/or added in extra.

Option A: Pair up partners in groups of four. Have each person tell the story to their small group.

Option B: Ask if anyone would like to tell the story to the whole group, with or without using their storyboard to assist them.

Favorite Part

This is a round activity using the talking piece.

What is your favorite part of this story today? Or the part that got your attention? If you like, show us your storyboard. You could let us know how you and your partner did telling it.

Connections

In this story the disciples are afraid of the religious authorities who had Jesus arrested and crucified, so they are hiding out in a room behind locked doors. The story invites us to consider a time we locked or barricaded doors because we were afraid.

In this story, the evening after God raised Jesus from the dead, he appears to his disciples behind locked doors. They rejoiced when they experienced his presence. So the story invites us to consider a time we experienced the presence of the risen Christ.

Winding Up

Check-Out/Feedback

In a round, invite participants to:

1. Give a word or phrase that describes how they are feeling now.
2. Give feedback on the Circle session.

Prayer Cards

If your church has a prayer ministry that has agreed to pray for your Circle participants, explain the ministry and invite participants to make prayer cards.

If you are able to make one-on-one visits, this is also a time to announce that as a possibility; suggest they write "visit" on their card.

Offer to write for anyone who would like to dictate their prayer request.

Collection

Gather all the items in the Circle and those passed out which need to be returned.

Closing

Standing in the Circle, conclude with "Go Now in Peace." Teach the ASL signs along with the words and tune before singing through as a group.

10

Conclusions and Possibilities

CIRCLE OF THE WORD implements the reconception of the Bible as performance literature to be internalized, embodied, and re-presented. This perspective contrasts with the modern assumption that the Bible is a text to be studied for information about history, science, theology, or even spirituality. Rather than Bible *study*, Circle of the Word is Bible *engagement*. Relating to the Bible as experience, rather than doctrine, offers a promising approach to the pursuit of restorative justice. Participants learn, tell, and interact with biblical stories through a variety of creative activities. They get background on the stories in their ancient context, and they reflect on connections between biblical stories and their lives today.

The connections are not forced. They often surface spontaneously; they easily emerge with the slightest encouragement. Biblical literature recalls the experience of oppression and enslavement in Egypt, captivity in Babylon, and subjugation by the Romans. In each instance, the stories that were generated in that period connect deeply with the experience of incarcerated persons now. Through Circle of the Word, participants relate with specific characters in the history of Israel. Upon hearing the story of Ezekiel in the valley of dry bones, one woman immediately responded, "I wish God would do that for me!"

The stories also connect us with the early Jesus movement, as does the story of Jesus' appearance to his disciples behind locked doors. Engaging that story inspired the comment, "This class is like a breath of fresh air."

These two stories about the Spirit's breath then, recalled for us in Ezekiel and John, become a breath of fresh air for people now.

Circle of the Word continues the historically transformative work of Elizabeth Fry and the early reformers of the penal system in England. The Society for Promoting Christian Knowledge began the call for prison reform and the effort to connect prisoners with the Bible. John Wesley and the Methodists preached grace, offering hope in situations of despair. Grounded in the stories of Jesus' actions and teachings, John Howard and Elizabeth Fry worked sacrificially to address the horrendous conditions of inhumanity and injustice involving imprisonment. They serve as inspiration for the work that needs to be done in our day.

Despite formidable obstacles, including gender prejudice, Elizabeth Fry made a significant difference in her own time with work that had lasting impact. The obstacles to dismantling mass incarceration in the United States are no less daunting. The memoirs of Elizabeth Fry bear witness to the power of biblical story when engaged at an experiential level. Both her words and her actions demonstrate the kind of spirit needed for this work: a spirit of humility, kindness, and compassion, while at the same time one of courage and perseverance.

These spiritual dynamics reflect the Word of God. This book proposes a new approach to engagement with the Bible as Word of God in the jails and prisons of the United States. Circle of the Word is a test and a potential confirmation of the transformative effect of the Word of God on individuals and groups. There is a uniquely powerful openness to encountering the Word of God when people become immersed in the details of specific biblical stories, approaching them from different angles and striving to learn them by heart. In the context of orality and safe community, focused engagement with the biblical Word of God is accompanied by the presence of the living Word of God.

For this reason, biblical stories have been a source of courage, guidance, and hope for many people in many times and places. This book confirms that they can be for people in our time as well, specifically in places of detention in our communities. Positive engagement with biblical stories lends itself to positive psychology. Circle of the Word is an exploration of the possibility that learning and telling biblical stories with incarcerated men and women can generate hope. It strives to open their world to new possibilities. It provides visions of pathways toward those new possibilities. It can be a source of strength for dealing with roadblocks and for empowerment to persevere toward goals. In short, Circle of the Word can stimulate hopeful thinking, a transcendent value of immense worth.

New possibilities also emerge in relation to the topic of this book. *A Breath of Fresh Air: Biblical Storytelling with Prisoners* explores and advocates a specific pedagogical approach to address a specific social concern. This particular implementation of the Bible as performance literature to be learned by heart and explored by storytelling processes can be implemented in a variety of settings. And it can be further developed in the context of prison ministry. I will identify some of those possibilities.

It may have occurred to you already that Circle of the Word is a viable approach to Bible engagement in settings other than jails and prisons. This is so true. Circle of the Word grew out of many years of experiential engagement with biblical stories in a wide range of venues with children, youth, and adults in diverse cultures. Certainly the methods proposed here could be adapted to any setting where a small group comes together for spiritual empowerment. Possibilities include local churches, camps, schools, recreation centers, and senior centers.

Performance criticism approaches to biblical study can be implemented in various contexts. Both in the wider contexts and in prison contexts the performance dimension can be cultivated. Returning our focus to the detention setting, let us imagine how Circle of the Word might lead a group of prisoners to provide an evening performance of their favorite biblical stories or a set of biblical stories based on a particular theme. They might weave together a biblical story with a personal story, naming significant connections between the two. At Christmas and Easter a group might learn and tell stories to the prison population in mini-epic style, integrating story and music in a performance venue.

Another direction to take Circle of the Word in a detention setting would be its adaptation for use with small group devotions. The men or women might learn a story a week, or perhaps a story a month. They might journal about their reflections on learning and telling the story and share them as a way of leading devotions. They might express their responses through artwork in whatever media they have available.

A Circle of the Word program might pursue more in-depth engagement with a particular story than one session allows. Participants could easily work with any biblical story for multiple sessions exploring its original context, its connection with their lives, and its performance.[1] They might develop their own resource based on that story to share with a wider audience inside and perhaps also outside the prison.

In a prison context where you have a stable group over an extended period of time, there is the opportunity to try things like a performance for the larger community or extended study of a particular story. In a jail, with its constantly changing population and even greater restrictions than in prison, those options are not as likely. Worship services, however, could easily adapt biblical storytelling, experiential preaching, and Circle of the Word principles for use in jail settings as well as in prison.

One final possibility that I can envision involves training "inside" leaders for biblical storytelling and Circle of the Word. The goal would be to develop a training program for empowering people with long-term sentences to tell biblical stories, to teach biblical stories, and to lead Circle of the Word sessions. This would give them a meaningful ministry and a way of extending God's Word to a lot more people than can be done by any one person. That being said, I have noticed time and again incarcerated men and women sharing the Word of God with their peers as a result of their participation in Circle of the Word without additional training.

A final story—"The Bent-Over Woman" (Luke 13:10–17) was the focus of our Circle in the jail one Wednesday afternoon in the summer of 2016. Twelve women came that day, our maximum number. It was an exceptionally enthusiastic group, with spontaneous comments: "I love this class!" and "I'm going to use these techniques with my grandchildren," and "This is my favorite program." One of the two newcomers said she came because everyone had told her what a great class it was. I laughed and said the pressure was really on, and that I hoped it lived up to her high expectations.

We learned the story about the woman who had been kept in bondage by a spirit of affliction for eighteen long years. She was bent-over and quite unable to stand up straight until Jesus set her free. We wrote down phrases from the story that especially got our attention and read around the Circle to understand more about synagogue, Sabbath, and Satan. We had some lively discussion about Sabbath practices then and now. We created storyboards and told the story to a partner. A couple of women used their storyboard to tell the story to the whole Circle.

---

1. This model of biblical storytelling with prisoners has been practiced by Dr. Joyce Johnson for a number of years at the Indiana Women's Prison in Indianapolis.

Then we began our Connections rounds. The first suggestion was: "Tell about a time you felt bent-over." I started by telling about the ending of my first marriage. Others shared; there were a few passes. The connection surfaced painful memories and hard struggles. About halfway around the Circle, a woman told about her long-term affliction, then started to talk about hope. With increasing emotion she exhorted us to have hope: "Don't ever lose hope, no matter what has happened, no matter what you have done. You always have hope. As long as you have breath, you have hope."[2] Her speech was eloquent and passionate.

The talking piece continued around the Circle with more hard-to-hear stories of being bent-over. There was complete silence when the talking piece found its way back to me. As sometimes happened I wondered if I had done a disservice calling up so much hardship to the surface. I had no choice at this point but to trust the story. I invited the women to hear it again and to allow it to wrap around and hold their memories.

After the telling we had a second round. I asked, "Like the woman who was set free, who stood up straight and began praising God, what do you praise God for today?" I began: "I praise God for my son giving me a call yesterday and that he's okay." Every woman in the Circle, without hesitation, followed with an "I praise God for" statement.

Circle of the Word is a simple intervention that weakens the grip of mass incarceration on our nation. It is, for me and for others, a breath of fresh air. The Gospel of John tells us that the resurrected Jesus breathed on his disciples and then told them. "Receive the Holy Spirit."

So . . . Don't forget to breathe.

---

2. Told with permission.

Bibliography

Alexander, Michelle. *The New Jim Crow: Mass Incarceration in the Age of Colorblindness.* New York: New Press, 2010.

Allard, Pierre and Wayne Northey "Christianity: The Rediscovery of Restorative Justice." In *The Spiritual Roots of Restorative Justice,* edited by Michael L. Hadley, 119–41. Albany: State University of New York Press, 2001.

Allen, W. O. B., and Edmund McClure. *Two Hundred Years: The History of the Society of Promoting Christian Knowledge.* London: SPCK, 1898.

Armour, Marilyn Peterson, Liliane Cambraia Windsor, Jemel Aguilar, Crystal Taub. "A Pilot Study of a Faith-Based Restorative Justice Intervention for Christian and Non-Christian Offenders." *Journal of Psychology and Christianity* 27 (2008) 159–67.

Asamoah-Gyadu, Kwabena and Peter Horsfield. "What Is It About the Book? Semantic and Material Dimensions in the Meditation of the Word of God." *Studies in World Christianity* 17 (2011) 175–93.

Baker, Frank. *The Works of John Wesley.* 25: *Letters I, 1721–1739.* Oxford: Clarendon, 1980.

Barth, Karl. *Church Dogmatics,* I/1: *The Doctrine of the Word of God.* Translated by G. T. Thomson et al. Edinburgh: T. & T. Clark, 1936.

———*The Epistle to the Romans.* 2nd ed. Translated by Edwyn C. Hoskyns from the 6th ed. 1933. Reprinted, London: Oxford University Press, 1968.

Battelle, L. G. *Pilgrims of Grace.* Nashville: Methodist Publishing, 1949.

Bellarmine, Robert. *Disputations about Controversies of the Christian Faith, Volume One, First General Controversy: On the Word of God, Written and Unwritten.* Translated by Peter L. P. Simpson, 2013. First published at Ingolstadt, 1581–1593. "Bellarmine's Disputations," Professor Peter L. P. Simpson, Aristotelophile. http://aristotelophile. com/current.htm.

Bellingham, David. *An Introduction to Greek Mythology.* London: Quintet, 1989.

Blackwood, Andrew W. Jr. *Ezekiel: Prophecy of Hope.* Grand Rapids: Baker, 1965.

Blenkinsopp, Joseph. *Ezekiel* Interpretation. Louisville: John Knox, 1990.

Boomershine, Thomas E. "Audience Address and Purpose in the Performance of Mark." In *Mark as Story: Retrospect and Prospect,* edited by Kelly R. Iverson and Christopher W. Skinner, 115–42. Atlanta: Society of Biblical Literature, 2011.

———. "The Medium and Message of John: Audience Address and Audience Identity in the Fourth Gospel." In *The Fourth Gospel in First-Century Media Culture,* edited by Anthony LeDonne and Tom Thatcher, 92–120. London: T. & T. Clark, 2011.

———. *The Messiah of Peace: A Performance Criticism Commentary on Mark's Passion-Resurrection Narrative.* Biblical Performance Criticism Series 12. Eugene, OR: Cascade Books, 2015.

———. *Story Journey: An Invitation to the Gospel as Storytelling.* Nashville: Abingdon, 1988.

———. "A Storytelling Commentary on John 20:19–31." GoTell Communications. http://gotell.org/wp-content/uploads/2015/06/Jn20_19–31_commentary.pdf.

Bopp, Linus. "The Salvific Power of the Word according to the Church Fathers." In *The Word: Readings in Theology.* New York: Kenedy, 1964.

Botha, Eugene, dir. *Orality, Print Culture and Biblical Interpretation.* Written, directed, filmed, and produced by Eugene Botha, 2013. MP4 video, 52:51. http://www.biblicalperformancecriticism.org/index.php/component/content/article/47-performance-video/236-orality-print-culture-and-biblical-interpretation-video.

Boyes-Watson, Carolyn, and Kay Pranis, eds. *Heart of Hope Resource Guide: Using Peacemaking Circles to Develop Emotional Literacy, Promote Healing, and Build Healthy Relationships.* Boston: Center for Restorative Justice at Suffolk University, 2010.

Boyle, Gregory. *Tattoos on the Heart: The Power of Boundless Compassion.* New York: Free Press, 2010.

Bradt, Kevin M., S.J. *Story as a Way of Knowing.* Kansas City: Sheed & Ward, 1976.

Bratcher, Robert G., and Eugene A. Nida. *A Translator's Handbook on the Gospel of Mark.* New York: United Bible Societies, 1961.

Bright, John. *A History of Israel.* Third ed. Philadelphia: Westminster, 1972.

Brown, Raymond E. *The Gospel according to John (XIII–XXI).* Anchor Bible 29A. Garden City, NY: Doubleday, 1970.

Burnside, Jonathan, Nancy Loucks, Joanna R. Adler and Gerry Rose. *My Brother's Keeper: Faith-Based Units in Prisons.* Portland, OR: Willan, 2005.

Butcher, H. Maxwell. *Story as a Way to God.* San Jose: Resource Publications, 1991.

Campbell, Joan. *The Ministry to the Imprisoned.* Collegeville, MN: Liturgical, 1989.

Cheavens, Jennifer S., David B. Feldman, Amber Gum, Scott T. Michael, and C. R. Snyder. "Hope Therapy in a Community Sample: A Pilot Investigation." *Social Indicators Research*, no. 77 (2006) 61–78.

Clifford, Richard J. "The Gift of the Word: The Achievements and Challenges of Vatican II on Scripture." *America: The National Catholic Weekly* 209.14 (Nov. 11, 2013) 14–19.

Clune, Erin Elizabeth. "House of Corrections: Lessons from Behind Bars." *America* (Sept. 1–8, 2014) 30–32.

Cody, Aelred. *Ezekiel: with an Excursus on Old Testament Priesthood.* Old Testament Message 11. Wilmington, DE: Glazier, 1984.

Cohn, Michael A. and Barbara L. Fredrickson. "Positive Emotions." In *Oxford Handbook of Positive Psychology,* edited by C.R. Snyder and Shane J. Lopez, 13–24. Oxford: Oxford University Press, 2009.

Collins, Adela Yarbro. *Mark: A Commentary.* Hermeneia. Minneapolis: Fortress, 2007.

Cone, James H. *The Cross and the Lynching Tree.* Maryknoll, NY: Orbis, 2011.

Cranton, Patricia. *Professional Development as Transformative Learning.* San Francisco: Jossey-Bass, 1996.

Creswell, John W. *Research Design: Qualitative, Quantitative, And Mixed Methods Approaches,* 4th ed. Los Angeles: Sage, 2014.

Dewey, Dennis. "Paper for the Seminar on Biblical Storytelling and Scholarship." 2004.

———. "Performing the Living Word." In *The Bible in Ancient and Modern Media: Story and Performance*, edited by Holly E. Hearon and Philip Ruge-Jones, 142–155. Biblical Performance Criticism Series 1. Eugene, OR: Cascade Books, 2009.

Diaz, George (Leo). "Breathing the Breath of Education on Those Ol' Dry Bones." In *Voices of the Class of 1998*, edited by friends of the New York Theological Seminary program at Sing Sing. New York: New York Theological Seminary, 1998.

Dickinson, Emily. *The Complete Poems of Emily Dickinson*. Boston: Little, Brown, 1924; Bartleby.com, 2000. www.bartleby.com/113/.

Diener, Ed. "Positive Psychology: Past, Present, and Future." In *Oxford Handbook of Positive Psychology*, edited by C. R. Snyder and Shane J. Lopez, 7–11. Oxford: Oxford University Press, 2009.

Duffy, Maria. *Paul Ricoeur's Pedagogy of Pardon: A Narrative Theory of Memory and Forgetting*. New York: Continuum, 2009.

Ebeling, Gerhard. *Word and Faith*. Translated by James W. Leitch. Philadelphia: Fortress, 1963.

Edwards, Denis. *Human Experience of God*. New York: Paulist, 1983.

Eicher, David, ed. *Glory to God: The Presbyterian Hymnal*. Louisville: Presbyterian Publishing, 2013.

Ekblad, Bob. *Reading the Bible with the Damned*. Louisville: Westminster John Knox, 2005.

Ellison, Gregory C., II. *Cut Dead but Still Alive: Caring for African American Young Men*. Nashville: Abingdon, 2013.

Ewart, David. "It's 'Judeans' not 'Jews.'" Holy Textures: Meeting Jesus in Matthew, Mark, Luke, and John. http://www.holytextures.com/its-judeans-not-jews.html.

Farrar, Mrs. John. *John Howard*. 1: *Lives of Philanthropists*, edited by Henry Ware, Jr. Cambridge, MA: Brown, Shattuck, 1833.

"The Fourth Report of the Committee of the Society for the Improvement of Prison Discipline and for the Reformation of Juvenile Offenders." London: Bensley, 1822.

Frei, Hans W. *The Eclipse of Biblical Narrative*. New Haven: Yale University Press, 1974.

Fry, Elizabeth. "Observations on the Visiting, Superintending, and Government of Female Prisoners." London: Arch, 1827.

Fry, Katherine, and Rachel Cresswell, eds. *Memoir of the Life of Elizabeth Fry with Extracts from Her Journal and Letters*. Philadelphia: Moore, 1847.

Funk, Robert W. *Language, Hermeneutic, and Word of God: The Problem of Language in the New Testament and Contemporary Theology*. New York: Harper & Row, 1966.

Gamble, Harry Y. *Books and Readers in the Early Church: A History of Early Christian Texts*. New Haven: Yale University Press, 1995.

Gardner, Howard. *Frames of Mind: The Theory of Multiple Intelligences*. 2nd ed. New York: Basic Books, 2004.

Garland, Hugh A. *The Life of John Randolph of Roanoke*. Vol. 2. 11th ed. New York: Haskell House, 1969. First published 1856.

Giblet, Jean. "The Johannine Theology of the *Logos*." In *The Word: Readings in Theology*, 104–46. New York: Kenedy, 1964.

Gibson, Edgar C. S. *John Howard*. Boston: Knight & Millet, 1902.

Glaze, Lauren E., and Danielle Kaeble. "Correctional Populations in the United States, 2013." Bureau of Justice Statistics Bulletin NCJ 248479. Office of Justice Programs, U.S. Department of Justice: December 2014. http://www.bjs.gov/index.cfm?ty=pbdetail&iid=5177.

Hadley, Michael L. *The Spiritual Roots of Restorative Justice*. Albany: State University of New York Press, 2001.

Hatton, Jean. *Betsy: The Dramatic Biography of Prison Reformer Elizabeth Fry*. Oxford: Monarch, 2005.

Hearon, Holly E., and Philip Ruge-Jones, eds. *The Bible in Ancient and Modern Media: Story and Performance*. Biblical Performance Criticism Series 1. Eugene, OR: Cascade Books, 2009.

Heavner, Betsey. *Congregational Tool Box for Prison Ministry*. Nashville: Discipleship Resources, 2007.

Heitzenrater, Richard P. *Wesley and the People Called Methodists*. Nashville: Abingdon, 1995.

Hess, Lisa. *Artisanal Theology: Intentional Formation in Radically Covenantal Companionship*. Eugene, OR: Cascade Books, 2009.

Hoffman, Mark G. Vitalis. "The Bible as Word of God." *Word & World* 32 (2012) 348–55.

Horsfield, Peter and Kwabena Asamoah-Gyadu. "What is it about the Book? Semantic and Material Dimensions in the Mediation of the Word of God." *Studies in World Christianity* 17 (2011) 175–93.

Howard, John. *The State of the Prisons in England and Wales, with Preliminary Observations, and an Account of Some Foreign Prisons*. London: William Eyres, 1777.

"Importance of Sabbath Schools." New York: Tract Society of the Methodist Episcopal Church, c. 1839–1869.

Iverson, Kelly R., and Christopher W. Skinner, eds. *Mark as Story: Retrospect and Prospect*. SBL Resources for Biblical Study 65. Atlanta: Society of Biblical Literature, 2011.

Jarecki, Eugene, dir. *The House I Live In*. Produced by Eugene Jarecki, 2012. Virgil Films, 2013. DVD.

Johnson, Byron R. *More God Less Crime: Why Faith Matters and How It Could Matter More*. West Conshohocken, PA: Templeton, 2011.

Jorns, Auguste, Dr. Rer. Pol. *The Quakers as Pioneers in Social Work*. Translated by Thomas Kite Brown, Jr. Port Washington, NY: Kennikat, 1931.

"The Journal of Charles Wesley." Wesley Center Online. http://wesley.nnu.edu/charles-wesley/the-journal-of-charles-wesley-1707–1788/the-journal-of-charles-wesley-january-2-february-27–1743/.

Kelsey, Morton T. "Listening." *Faith at Work* (Fall 1995) 12–13.

Kent, John. *Elizabeth Fry*. New York: Arco, 1963.

Kerman, Piper. *Orange Is the New Black: My Year in a Women's Prison*. New York: Spiegel & Grau, 2011.

King, Martin Luther, Jr. *Strength to Love*. Minneapolis: Fortress, 2010.

Latourelle, Rene. "Revelation, History and Incarnation." In *The Word: Readings in Theology*, 27–63. New York: Kenedy, 1964.

Lee, Margaret Ellen, and Bernard Brandon Scott. *Sound Mapping the New Testament*. Salem, OR: Polebridge, 2009.

Leonard, Augustin. "Toward a Theology of the Word of God." In *The Word: Readings in Theology*, 64–89. New York: Kenedy, 1964.

Levad, Amy. *Redeeming a Prison Society: Response to Mass Incarceration*. Minneapolis: Fortress, 2014.

Logan, James Samuel. *Good Punishment? Christian Moral Practice and U.S. Imprisonment*. Grand Rapids: Eerdmans, 2008.

Lopez, Shane J., and Matthew W. Gallagher. "A Case for Positive Psychology." In *Oxford Handbook of Positive Psychology*, edited by C. R. Snyder and Shane J. Lopez, 3–6. Oxford: Oxford University Press, 2009.

Magness, Jodi. *Stone and Dung, Oil and Spit: Jewish Daily Life in the Time of Jesus.* Grand Rapids: Eerdmans, 2011.

Malina, Bruce J., and Richard L. Rohrbaugh. *Social-Science Commentary on the Gospel of John.* Minneapolis: Fortress, 1998.

Marcus, Joel. *Mark 1–8.* Anchor Bible 27. New York: Doubleday, 2000.

Marshall, Christopher. *Beyond Retribution: A New Testament Vision for Justice, Crime, and Punishment.* Grand Rapids: Eerdmans, 2001.

Maslow, Abraham H. *Motivation and Personality.* New York: Harper, 1954.

Maxey, James A. *From Orality to Orality: A New Paradigm for Contextual Translation of the Bible.* Biblical Performance Criticism Series 2. Eugene, OR: Cascade Books, 2009.

McKeating, Henry. *Ezekiel.* Old Testament Guides. Sheffield: Sheffield Academic, 1993.

McLaren, Brian D. *Why Did Jesus, Moses, the Buddha, and Mohammed Cross the Road?: Christian Identity in a Multi-Faith World.* New York: Jericho, 2012.

Menninger, Karl. "The Academic Lecture on Hope." *American Journal of Psychiatry* 116 (1959) 481–91.

Miles, Matthew B., A. Michael Huberman, and Johnny Saldaña. *Qualitative Data Analysis: A Methods Sourcebook.* 3rd ed. Los Angeles: Sage, 2014.

"A Murderer's Deathbed." New York: Tract Society of the Methodist Episcopal Church, 19th century.

Navone, John, S.J. *Seeking God in Story.* Collegeville, MN: Liturgical, 1990.

Navone, John, S.J., and Thomas Cooper. *Tellers of the Word.* New York: Le Jacq, 1981.

Nelson, Fred. *Spiritual Survival Guide.* Park Ridge, IL: Under the Door, 2012.

Nordquist, Richard. "About Education." September 26, 2014. http://grammar.about.com/od/fh/g/histpreterm.htm.

Northey, Wayne. "Restorative Justice Vision and Spirituality." ARPA (Association for Reformed Political Action) presentation, Langley Canadian Reformed Church, March 5, 2005. http://waynenorthey.com/wp-content/uploads/2014/02/restorative-justice-arpa-march-5-2005.pdf.

Northrup, Solomon. *Twelve Years a Slave.* New York: Miller, Orton & Mulligan, 1855.

Nürnberger, Klaus. *Martin Luther's Message for Us Today: A Perspective from the South.* Pietermaritzburg: Cluster, 2005.

Ong, Walter J. *Orality and Literacy: The Technologizing of the Word.* New York: Methuen, 1982.

————*The Presence of the Word: Some Prolegomena for Cultural and Religious History.* New Haven: Yale University Press, 1967.

Pace, Dale K. *A Christian's Guide to Effective Jail & Prison Ministries.* Old Tappan, NJ: Revell, 1976.

Parker, Theodore. *Ten Sermons of Religion* (1857). Quoted by Garson O'Toole in "The Arc of the Moral Universe Is Long But It Bends Toward Justice" (blog). http://quoteinvestigator.com/2012/11/15/arc-of-universe.

Peterson, Christopher, and Martin E. P. Seligman. *Character Strengths and Virtues: A Handbook and Classification.* New York: Oxford University Press, 2004.

Pierce, Dennis W. *Prison Ministry: Hope Behind the Wall.* New York: Haworth Pastoral, 2006.

Bibliography

Pilgrims of Grace. Vol. 2, *A History of Grace United Methodist Church of Dayton, Ohio 1948 to 1976.*

Pranis, Kay. *The Little Book of Circle Processes: A New/Old Approach to Peacemaking.* Intercourse, PA: Good Books, 2005.

Pringle, Patrick. *The Prisoners' Friend: The Story of Elizabeth Fry.* New York: Roy, 1954.

"The Radicals of the Reformation." WWW-VL History Central Catalogue. European University Institute, Florence, Italy. http://vlib.iue.it/carrie/texts/carrie_books/gilbert/15.html.

Rand, Kevin L., and Jennifer S. Cheavens. "Hope Theory." In *Oxford Handbook of Positive Psychology,* edited by C. R. Snyder and Shane J. Lopez, 323–33. Oxford: Oxford University Press, 2009.

Redmond, Marybeth Christie, and Sarah W. Bartlett, eds. *Hear Me See Me: Incarcerated Women Write.* Maryknoll, NY: Orbis, 2013.

Reid, Mark K. "On Identifying the Word of God Today." *Lexington Theological Quarterly* 10 (1975) 7–18.

Renner, Johannes. "The Word of God, Church, and Theology Today." *Lutheran Theological Journal* 16 (1982) 129–37.

Rhoads, David. "Performance Criticism: An Emerging Methodology in Second Testament Studies—Part I." *Biblical Theology Bulletin* 36 (2006) 118–33. http://www.biblicalperformancecriticism.org/index.php/2011-08-26-20-28-44/articles-mainmenu-37/articles/3-performance-criticism-an-emerging-discipline-part-i/file.

———. "Performance Events in Early Christianity: New Testament Writings in an Oral Context." In *The Interface of Orality and Writing: Speaking, Seeing, Writing in the Shaping of New Genres,* edited by Annette Weissenrieder and Robert B. Coote, 166–93. 2010. Reprinted, Biblical Performance Criticism Series 11. Eugene, OR: Cascade Books, 2015.

———. "What Is Performance Criticism?" In *The Bible in Ancient and Modern Media: Story and Performance,* edited by Holly E. Hearon and Philip Ruge-Jones, 83–100. Biblical Performance Criticism Series 1. Eugene, OR: Cascade Books, 2009.

Richert, Scott P. "Pope Francis: 'The Word of God Preceded the Bible and Surpasses It.'" *About Religion.* http://catholicism.about.com/b/2013/04/12/pope-francis-the-word-of-god-precedes-the-bible-and-surpasses-it.htm.

Ricoeur, Paul. *Figuring the Sacred: Religion, Narrative, and Imagination.* Minneapolis: Fortress, 1995.

———. *From Text to Action: Essays in Hermeneutics, II.* Evanston, IL: Northwestern University Press, 1991.

Rosenberg, Marshall B. *Nonviolent Communication: A Language of Life.* Encinitas, CA: Puddle Dancer, 2003.

Ruge-Jones, Philip. "Mentored into Steadfast Love." *The Living Pulpit* (August 2, 2013) http://www.pulpit.org.

———. "Storytelling and the Art of Teaching Theology." Texas Lutheran University, 2004.

Ryder, Edward. *Elizabeth Fry: Life and Labors of the Eminent Philanthropist, Preacher, and Prison Reformer.* New York: Walker, 1883.

Sample, Tex. *Hard Living People & Mainstream Christians.* Nashville: Abingdon, 1993.

Sanders, J. N., and B. A. Mastin. *A Commentary on the Gospel according to St. John.* Peabody, MA: Hendrickson, 1968.

Sawicki, Marianne. *The Gospel in History: Portrait of a Teaching Church, the Origins of Christian Education.* New York: Paulist, 1988.

———. *Seeing the Lord: Resurrection and Early Christian Practices*. Minneapolis: Fortress, 1994.

Schaff, Philip. *A Select Library of the Nicene and Post-Nicene Fathers of the Christian Church*. Edited by Philip Schaff. Buffalo: Christian Literature, 1886. 1: *The Confessions and Letters of St. Augustin, with a Sketch of His Life and Work*. http://oll.libertyfund.org/titles/1903#Schaff_1330-01_1563.

Schillebeeckx, Edward. "Revelation in Word and Deed." In *The Word: Readings in Theology*, 255–72. New York: Kenedy, 1964.

"Search the Scriptures." New York: Tract Society of the Methodist Episcopal Church, 19th century.

Senghor, Shaka. *Writing My Wrongs: Life, Death, and Redemption in an American Prison*. New York: Convergent, 2016.

Shiner, Whitney. *Proclaiming the Gospel: First-Century Performance of Mark*. Harrisburg, PA: Trinity, 2003.

Snyder, C. R., ed. *Handbook of Hope: Theory, Measures, and Applications*. San Diego: Academic, 2000.

———. "Hypothesis: There Is Hope." In *Handbook of Hope: Theory, Measures, and Applications* edited by C. R. Snyder, 3–21. San Diego: Academic, 2000.

Snyder, C. R., and Shane J. Lopez. *Oxford Handbook of Positive Psychology*. Oxford: Oxford University Press, 2009.

Social Principles of the UMC. http://www.umc.org/what-we-believe/political-community.

Soggin, J. Alberto. *Introduction to the Old Testament: From Its Origins to the Closing of the Alexandrian Canon*. Rev. ed. Philadelphia: Westminster, 1974.

Sprague, C. Joseph. "That Which Is Good and Required of Grace to Enter God's Preferred Future." Paper presented at the 200th Anniversary Celebration Luncheon of Grace United Methodist Church, Dayton, OH, September 25, 2011.

Stevenson, Bryan. *Just Mercy: A Story of Justice and Redemption*. New York: Spiegel & Grau, 2014.

Tabor, Margaret E. *Pioneer Women: Elizabeth Fry, Elizabeth Blackwell, Florence Nightingale, Mary Slessor*. London: Sheldon, 1925.

Thatcher, Tom, ed. *Memory and Identity in Ancient Judaism and Early Christianity: A Conversation with Barry Schwartz*. Semeia Studies Series 78. Atlanta: SBL, 2014.

Tiffany, Frederick C., and Sharon H. Ringe. *Biblical Interpretation: A Roadmap*. Nashville: Abingdon, 1996.

Tillich, Paul. *Systematic Theology*. Vol. 1. Chicago: University of Chicago Press, 1951.

Todd, John M. *Luther: A Life*. New York: Crossroad, 1982.

Tomkins, Stephen. *John Wesley: A Biography*. Grand Rapids: Eerdmans, 2003.

Toulouse, Mark G. "Christian Responses to Vietnam: The Organization of Dissent." Religion and Culture Web Forum (June 2007). https://divinity.uchicago.edu/sites/default/files/imce/pdfs/webforum/062007/vietnam.pdf.

Umbreit, Mark, and Marilyn Peterson Armour. *Restorative Justice Dialogue: An Essential Guide for Research and Practice*. New York: Springer, 2011.

Ward, Richard F., and David J. Trobisch. *Bringing the Word to Life: Engaging the New Testament through Performing It*. Grand Rapids: Eerdmans, 2013.

Weissenrieder, Annette, and Robert B. Coote, ed. *The Interface of Orality and Writing: Speaking, Seeing, Writing in the Shaping of New Genres*. 2010. Reprinted, Biblical Performance Criticism Series 11. Eugene, OR: Cascade Books, 2015.

Bibliography

Wesley, Charles. *The Journal of the Rev. Charles Wesley, M.A.* Vol. 1. Grand Rapids: Baker, 1980.

Whitaker, William. *A Disputation on Holy Scripture: Against the Papists, Especially Bellarmine and Stapleton.* Translated and edited by William Fitzgerald. Cambridge: Cambridge University Press, 1849.

Wicklund, Carl. "Hope in Community Corrections: Why Bother?" *Perspectives* (Summer, 2000) 18–22.

Williams, Timothy. "A '90s Legacy That Is Filling Prisons Today." *New York Times*, July 5, 2016, A1, A11.

Wink, Walter. *The Bible in Human Transformation.* Philadelphia: Fortress, 1973.

———. *Engaging the Powers: Discernment and Resistance in a World of Domination.* Minneapolis: Fortress, 1992.

———. *Homosexuality and the Bible.* Nyack, NY: Fellowship, 1996.

Zehr, Howard. *Changing Lenses: A New Focus for Crime and Justice.* Scottdale, PA: Herald, 1990.

———. *The Little Book of Restorative Justice.* Intercourse, PA: Good Books, 2002.

Zimmerli, Walther. *Ezekiel 2: A Commentary on the Book of the Prophet Ezekiel Chapters 25–48.* Translated by Ronald E. Clements. Hermeneia. Philadelphia: Fortress, 1983.

Made in the USA
Coppell, TX
02 August 2020